Acknowledgements

My deeply grateful thanks are due to several colleagues who gave generously of their time in debating these issues with me. They are: Professor Tony Allcock, Dr Tim Blackman, Dr Bill Carter, Professor Peter Daws, Sandra Griffiths, Dr Ken Houston, John McAleer, Mike Morrissey, Pauline Murphy, Dr Rhona Newman, and Professor Bill Watts. Dialogue with each of them, possessing as they do sharp and coherent ideas about university education, was an invaluable stimulation in helping me to confirm my own perspective. Andrea Henderson provided useful information about the careers advisory service and Roger Woodward helpfully made available relevant statistics.

In the practical but vital matters of typing, editing on the word processor and assistance with lay-out, I had the skilled assistance of my secretary, Mrs Madeleine Lynch. Her infinite patience, efficiency and moral support have had a considerable sustaining effect, and for all of this, I would like to record my heart-felt appreciaton.

Brian Caul

CONTENTS

VALUE-ADDED

The Personal Development of Students in Higher Education

Brian Caul

Published by December Publications
157 University Street, Belfast

© Brian Caul, 1993

ISBN 0 9517068 4 5

Printed by Graham & Heslip

Value-Added

The Personal Development of Students in Higher Education

Introduction

This book has been written at a time when higher education in the United Kingdom and Ireland is in a state of fascinating flux. The binary line between polytechnics and universities in the United Kingdom, a feature of the post-Robbins Report era since the 1960s, has now all but disappeared as the polytechnics have taken up the opportunity to adopt university status. In the Republic of Ireland, the former National Institutes of Higher Education, broadly similar to polytechnics in their aims, have also shiny new labels on their portals as the University of Limerick and Dublin City University.

However both national situations are dynamic in the sense that there is a rich admixture of traditions and values among and within the various universities, and indeed a healthy tension. The broad themes which contribute to this tension include: definitions of the roles which the respective institutions are or should be playing in relation to their societies; the balance between applied relevance in university courses and critical scholarship; and the extent to which universities can realistically increase access to a wide cross-section of learners and maintain quality at a time when resources from public funds are diminishing. Most institutions accept and applaud the governmental aspirations to increase the rates of participation in higher education, not only through conventional routes, but by showing more flexibility towards the needs and rights of 'second-chance' learners or people with special needs arising from disability or socio-economic circumstances. Undoubtedly, by the end of the present decade, even with the recent brake applied on expansion in the United Kingdom, there will have been a very substantial impact on the very social structure because of increased access in terms of the age and the social backgrounds of the students.

In the process of achieving these aims, genuine concerns are expressed by the academic tutors and the staff in the support services which have to be addressed. If increasing student numbers are not matched by additional staff resources, what impact will this have on the teaching contact hours demanded from academic tutors? Reciprocally, will larger populations lead to greater de-personalisation and less profound learning experiences? In this context, will academic freedom and the relative autonomy of universities be eroded, in the drive to meet the selective needs of the State for a trained and qualified work force? From the standpoint of support services, many questions arise, which it would be perilous to ignore. If future student populations are to be much more heterogeneous, what services will be provided to ensure that the wider range of needs is catered for, ranging from cultivation of suitable study skills, to provision of specialized equipment for students with disabilities? Given the current problems associated with lack of personal finance, how will future students be expected to realize their full potential unless the structure of income support is radically reviewed? Will 'reading' for a degree, in its literal sense of using well stocked libraries, be replaced by new uses of computer technology? In general are there dangers that mass higher education will lead to more shallow and superficial experiences for students and possibly more casualties who will not have easy access to appropriate support services?

While these key issues are rightly and properly put forward by concerned staff of universities, there is a general recognition of social and economic realities which confront them. Like every other major social institution, universities will have to demonstrate very lucidly in future that they are providing value for money. The arbiters of this will not just be the governments of the day, but the student consumers themselves, whose choice of courses will dictate whether particular universities earn sufficient revenue from tuition fees to flourish, or indeed survive. An essential part of this overt commitment to provide value for money, will be the increasing use of measures of the quality of teaching and support services. This subject in the past has provoked defensiveness, but more recently serious efforts have been made to establish appropriate performance indicators and modes of appraisal and evaluation of the individual performances of university staff.

At this point of great and challenging change, the following contents are meant to represent a celebration of higher education, an affirmation of its valuable role within society. Old 'sacred cows' are not held up in awe; rather there is an attempt to reflect critically on the historical context of university education. The origins of the European 'universitas' are examined, and the translation of its scholastic values into Britain and Ireland. With the Industrial Revolution, came the birth of the 'Redbricks', followed in turn by the ready-mix concrete and glass creations which heralded the Robbins era after the Second World War. Not only their charter dates but their expressed educational values will be considered, in terms of their relevance to modern higher education. Taking into account recent developments in relation to Government policy, consideration is then given as to what constitute valid functions and principles to be adopted by the universities of the future. As specific issues arising from this exposition, ideas will be presented on the ways and means of achieving wider access and provision of a reasonable and economic income support structure to ensure that the student population of tomorrow can benefit from that access without the corrosive endurance test of an inadequate budget.

The main thrust of this book emanates from the belief that universities should be offering opportunities for the personal development of students. As a result of their time on campus, their lives should be enriched not just through intellectual stimulation but also socially, emotionally and culturally. Rather than having a mechanistic factory processing role, universities should encourage the students to value the experience for its own sake. At the same time, students should be prepared for their departure with the skills and knowledge to take their places as useful if not always conventional citizens. This is the 'value-added' that universities can give, and one which is essential to the broader health and wellbeing of their societies. A substantial section of the book is devoted to an explication as to which support services are necessary to ensure that students have the means and resources available to promote their own personal development from a comprehensive accommodation service to a good careers advisory service, from a personal counselling and guidance service to a vibrant students' union or representative council.

In the concluding chapter, an effort is made to draw together the essential principles of practice which ensure an integrated approach to the personal development of students on the part of the Faculties and the support services. Finally, an illustration is presented of one possible method of measuring the 'value-added' of the university experience – a personal profile registering change on a number of levels of personal development which the student could not only prize for its own sake, but use effectively in the pursuit of a suitable future career.

Providing a bedrock for the ideas expressed in the book is the belief that higher education is primarily concerned with the pursuit of knowledge for its own sake. In the midst of temporal political ideologies or economic stringency, it is especially important that this flame of ultimate purpose continues to shine brightly. Higher education must be adaptable to new ideas and responsive to changing community needs. Nonetheless, the 'value-added' which universities should provide for individual people and for society as a whole, is freedom for critical reflection, questioning of assumptions and opportunities for comprehensive personal development. A healthy democracy needs such graduate citizens to invigorate and enrich it.

Chapter One

The Historical Context of
British and Irish Universities

The seeds of the University systems of Britain and Ireland were sown in the twelfth century. A time of great intellectual activity and regeneration, there were several developments which had a particularly significant influence on later educational advancement. Paramount features were the upsurge in the priority given to the study of canon law and Roman law; and the growing influence in Europe of Aristotelian logic. Up to this point, the most advanced learning took place in schools which formed part of monasteries or cathedrals but these tended to depend on the reputations of their encumbent teachers rather than having any consistent and coherent structures. Salerno is recognized as the first organized university, specializing in medicine. Of more widespread influence was the foundation in the second half of the twelfth century of the University of Bologna, the main fields of study of which were canon and Roman law.

However, it was to be the University of Paris, formed around 1170 and given a Charter and Papal recognition by 1231, which came to have the characteristics associated with later European universities. Just as tradesmen such as tailors or merchants had 'gilds', so scholars and teachers formed themselves for the purpose of self-protection and mutual benefit into 'universitas scholarium' and 'universitas magistrorum'. Bologna represented a 'universitas scholarium' where the students by dint of their healthy financial status employed and controlled the teachers. In contrast the University of Paris was established in the form of a 'universitas magistrorum' (Association of Masters), the model which was to be replicated later at Oxford. Another medieval term used to describe the universities was 'studium generale'. Whereas a 'studium' was any place of learning, a 'studium generale' admitted students from any nation and offered study in Arts and at least one other 'Faculty' of either Civil or Canon Law, or Medicine or Theology. Another distinctive feature of the medieval university was its autonomy as a corporate community with the right to govern itself and award its own degrees.

The lower Faculty of Arts and the four higher Faculties constituted the hierarchical framework for the teaching of the universities. The seven 'Liberal Arts', of Graeco-Roman origin consisted of the 'trivium' (grammar, logic and rhetoric) and the 'quadrivium' (music, astronomy, arithmetic and geometry). It was the normal expectation that the scholars would complete this form of foundation course or first degree before proceeding to the higher disciplines. Pedagogical practice was based on lectures and syllogistic 'disputation' grounded in Aristotelian logic. Dialectical ability was therefore a central requirement for the award of a degree, especially at Masters or Doctorate level. Self-sufficient independence was bestowed upon the universities by either sovereign rulers or the Pope.

> It is no exaggeration to say that the university was the greatest invention of the Middle Ages, and the most important legacy bequeathed by them to the modern world. (S J Curtis 1963 p 56.)

The British Medieval Universities

The British medieval university tradition was established at Oxford and Cambridge, which received papal recognition in 1214 and 1318 respectively. At Oxford the framework for education was similar to its predecessor, the University of Paris, in that it was derived from the Seven Liberal Arts. As discussed earlier these represented a foundation course, a necessary precursor which had to be undertaken successfully by students before they could graduate into the professional studies of law, medicine or theology. It would appear that the early students were particularly noted for their lawlessness and licentious behaviour. All male, they were often poor and could not afford either books or the fees due to their tutors – many left without taking a degree. At the same time the majority appeared to enjoy a lively and enthusiastic climate in which active and critical learning was encouraged. Indeed, fostered by the inviolate independence bestowed on the universities, there was an insatiable appetite for dispute and controversy. The prerogative of the intellectual to indulge in freedom of expression was greatly prized and defended against any possible state intervention even to the point of incurring civil commotion!

> The 'seculars', who regarded themselves as the University proper, consisted of secular clergy, priests like Wycliffe, or deacons and clerks in lower orders. These men were academicians first and churchmen second. They were as zealous for the 'liberties' of their University as a burgher for those of his town. They were always on guard against Papal and episcopal interference, royal mandates and the claims and privileges of the town. Their rights were defended against all aggression by the hosts of turbulent undergraduates herding in the squalid lodging-houses of Oxford, who,

> when occasion called, poured forth to threaten the life of the Bishop's messenger, to hoot the King's officials, or to bludgeon and stab the mob that maintained the Mayor against the Chancellor. (G M Trevelyan 1973 p.53.)

It is also on record that there were riots at Cambridge in 1381, during which townspeople destroyed the University's Charter and records!

Following an intervention by Henry III, Oxford and Cambridge had to ensure that all students' names were entered onto a role or 'matricula' of a particular regent master for the purposes of instruction, supervision and the avoidance of impostors. (J Lawson and H Silver 1973). At this stage, the universities were not providing for a social elite. In practice they were centres of professional training for teachers, clergy, lawyers and administrators. In addition they were not pursuing knowledge for its own sake or adopting research methodology in any modern sense. The social context was one where truth was believed to be found, not in scholarly inquiry and experiments, but rather in the scriptures or the adages of Greek philosophers. Logic and reason, questioning and disputation were the intellectual tools by which knowledge and truth was extracted from various texts of unimpeachable authority. (H C Barnard 1969 p 31.)

The Collegiate Ethos

In practice, the intellectual freedom of the universities in relation to religious and ecclesiastical issues came to be severely constrained in the late medieval period. However there was a rapid growth in a more disciplined and integrated collegiate life, which led to a civilized and moral ethos of widening influence among the wealthy gentry.

> The number of great Elizabethans who had been at Oxford or Cambridge is significant of a new attitude to learning in the government class. A gentleman, especially if he aspired to serve the State, would now finish his education at one of the 'learned Universities', whence he usually came away with a familiar knowledge of the Latin language and of classical mythology, a smattering of Greek, and a varying measure of mathematical and philosophical acquirements. (G M Trevelyan 1973 p.182.)

Barnard points to the death of Cardinal Wolsey in 1531, as the demise of the last great statesman-prelate. Kings before the Reformation had relied on legally trained ecclesiastics to provide their advice and counsel. Subsequently, the professional advisers of the monarchy tended to come from the ranks of peers and gentry who had some experience of scholarship in the universities. (H C Barnard 1969 p 144.)

The Scottish Universities

Up to the fifteenth century Scottish students seeking higher education often went to the European universities such as Bologna, Louvain, Pisa and Geneva. Indeed in the University of Padua, there were sufficient Scottish students to establish a 'nation'. And from 1326, an actual college had been established at the University of Paris specifically for Scottish students. Although some of the students did go to Oxford and Cambridge, the political relationship between England and Scotland was highly volatile at this time and travel between the two countries was by no means safe. However Balliol College at Oxford had been established by the eponymous benefactor in order to assist Scottish students on low incomes.

Supported by a general feeling that Scotland did need a university of its own, Bishop Wardlaw obtained a Papal Bull in 1413 to establish a 'studium generale' at St Andrews. Once again the University of Paris was used as a model and the incoming students were divided into 'Nations' according to their geographical locations. Beginning with very limited resources, both in terms of staff and buildings, St Andrews had inaugurated three colleges by the sixteenth century.

Another Papal Bull, inspired by the commitment of the Bishop of Glasgow, founded the University of Glasgow in 1451, a Royal Charter being granted by James II in 1453. The role models for this institution were the Universities of Bologna and Louvain. Completing the trilogy, the University of Aberdeen was established in 1494 by Papal Bull at the instigation of James IV and Bishop Elphinstone. The remoteness of this geographical area was emphasized to strengthen its case for a university and the Bishop ensured that it received substantial initial endowments which resulted in Aberdeen having a much more secure financial base in the early stages than the other Scottish universities.

With Edinburgh achieving university status in the sixteenth century, it is quite remarkable that Scotland had four formally constituted universities by this stage. In 1560 the population throughout Scotland was less than half a million and poverty was rampant. Yet all of these universities were to play a highly significant part in the intellectual and cultural development of people, not just from the United Kingdom but eventually from all over the world. (S J Curtis 1963.)

The First Colonial University

In 1591 Trinity College Dublin was founded by a Charter from Elizabeth I. Its constitution was closely modelled on that of Trinity College Cambridge, and its first three Provosts were alumni from Cambridge. In effect, the University of Dublin, as it came to be known, provided Irish students with educational opportunities which hitherto had to be sought in England.

> The real significance of the foundation of Trinity College is that it was the first colonial university institution, equipped to carry out the functions of both a college and a university, and as such the prototype of Harvard (1639), Yale (1701), Columbia (1734), and other institutions overseas.
>
> (N Atkinson 1969 p 36.)

Just as Oxford and Cambridge promoted the training of the clergy and the professional classes, Trinity College was created to inculcate the habits and religion of the English into the sons of the Irish upper classes. Student life in Trinity appears to have had features similar to those of the early days of Oxford and Cambridge, being described as:

> A sanctuary for debtors, a threat to any bailiffs who dared to encroach, avenging hordes who went armed with lethal weapons made out of room keys and handkerchiefs to avenge any insult to one of their members.
>
> (Dublin University Magazine XXI, 279.)

Trinity College, in accordance with the English universities, was a preserve for Anglicans. It was only under the authority of a Royal Letter in 1793 that Catholics could be admitted to study for degrees at its portals. However it was pronounced by the Bishops as an unsuitable place for the education of Roman Catholic clergymen because: it did not teach all the subjects required; clergymen were obliged to study in seminary residence; and Dublin was far too expensive and distracting!

Subsequently an Act of Parliament of 1795 established Maynooth College as an institution for the education of priests, with no restriction on the education of laymen. In 1845 it was decided to create new institutions of higher education in Ireland that would be undenominational and collegiate, and Queen's Colleges were set up at Belfast, Cork and Galway. (A separate and independent Magee College was established for Presbyterian clergy in 1865 at Londonderry.)

Decline and Criticism at Oxford and Cambridge

The Church of England continued to be the dominant influence in Oxford and Cambridge, aided and abetted by occasional state intervention such as the Test Act of 1673 which required all office-holders to take the sacraments according to the rites of the Church of England. In effect this meant that neither Roman Catholics nor Dissenters could teach at universities and this tended to stultify teaching standards and reinforce unimaginative conformity. (N Graves 1988 p 89.)

During the 1700s, the vast majority of students came from grammar schools of all kinds, with Eton and Westminster being particularly highly represented. As many as one in four of the students were provided by private tutors. Numbers in fact sank considerably in the 1750s and 1760s, at which point there had not been so few students for over 200 years. This situation improved somewhat towards the end of the century, as some colleges began to effect a more considered and serious approach to education. Pressure for reforms was growing at this time, particularly with a view to the abolition of religious tests, more searching degree examinations and the need for competitive elections for scholarships. The continual lobbying by liberal factions for administrative and academic improvements won the appointment of a Royal Commission in 1850, with whom Oxford and Cambridge refused to co-operate. Nonetheless criticisms of inefficiency in teaching, inadequate professorial arrangements and maladministration were accepted by the Commission and two Acts followed, one concerning Oxford in 1854 and the other Cambridge in 1856. These removed the bar on non-members of the Church of England in relation to bachelor's degrees (but not masters), reformed the scholarship system and opened fellowships to competition. Eventually the battle to abolish all religious tests and the Anglican Church's control over university government was won in 1871.

> An academic 'liberal' party, of great intellectual distinction and very much
> in earnest, fought the battle to free Oxford and Cambridge from the bondage
> of Church monopoly and won it by the Test Act of 1871. The younger
> universities of London and Manchester had long enjoyed such freedom as
> their birth right. (G M Trevelyan 1973 p 567.)

The Impact of the Industrial Revolution

With the onset of the industrial revolution, the university system developed really to provide knowledge intensive labour to facilitate the process of a society which was becoming more industrially complex. The system which emerged with the industrial revolution required a much higher and more extensive standard of administration and management. Reciprocally the universities within the British system were to be essential in providing these administrators.

> National needs were brought into focus by the Great Exhibition of 1851.
> The public began to realise that to maintain Britain's position as the
> workshop of the world it would be necessary to strengthen education in
> science and technology. The fear of industrial competition from the
> Continent was a powerful stimulus. There was increasing awareness of the
> success of the German universities, which subordinated all other functions
> to the concept of 'wissenschaft" – the university as a centre of research. The
> new civic universities absorbed 'wissenschaft' in their very foundation
> stones. (M Allen 1988 p 36.)

It is arguable that the growth of universities in the nineteenth century was a direct result of the inability or disinclination of Oxford and Cambridge to meet Britain's needs in terms of the industrial revolution. In contrast, the 'civic' universities such as Durham, Manchester and Birmingham were directly intended to address local needs as identified in their own geographical regions. (See Appendix I)

> The University is the handmaid of the State, of which it is the microcosm
> – a community in which also there are rulers and ruled, and in which the
> corporate life is a moulding influence. And so we arrive at the truth, which
> is becoming yearly more and more clearly perceived, not here alone, but in
> other lands, that the State must see to the wellbeing and equipment of its
> Universities, if it is to be furnished with the best quality in its citizens and
> in its servants. (Haldane 1912 p 93.)

In reviewing the growth of the institutions of higher education, Birch attempted to provide a balance between the pursuit of scholarship within universities and the dangers of a 'closed system' blinkered view of knowledge:

> The emergence of the university in mediaeval Europe as a physical and
> social expression of the scholarly community, was closely associated with
> the Church and with the preparation of students for the learned professions:
> law, medicine and the Church. The eventual and difficult separation of
> these universities from the Church was a notable contribution to the ethos
> of higher education, in the sense that it was a search for the freedom to
> pursue the truth unfettered by the dogma and therefore the constraints of the
> Church. (W Birch 1988 p 7.)

This statement illustrates how there was to be an in-built tension in defining the role of the universities in a twentieth century context. The concurrent issues which reflected this tension were the sincere belief of educationalists that protected freedom of thought was to the benefit of wider society, and the external reality that the world around the universities was rapidly changing and making demands. Trevelyan asserted the classical position of many academics on the subject of liberty.

> ...the essential liberty of the Universities, which had been infringed in
> various degrees by Tudors, Stuarts and Cromwellians, was established by
> Eighteenth Century practice. In some respects this unanimity was abused,
> but we may thank God that it was preserved, when we consider the state of
> slavery into which academic life has fallen in countries which had no such
> venerable tradition of the rule of law and the liberty of the subject.
>
> (G M Trevelyan 1973 p 367.)

Attempting to bridge the gap between the autonomy of the university and the needs of the state, Viscount Haldane laid grandiloquent emphasis on the pursuit of 'Truth'. He maintained that universities would not thrive if they were dependent institutions under church or state domination. The spirit which was their driving force required freedom for expression and development of ideas. Only the 'Truth' could command obedience and universities should not be compelled to recognize any other authority. (Haldane 1912 p 105.) However in his Rectorial Address to the University of Edinburgh in 1907, he coupled his sentiments with elitist aspirations promulgating the importance of a university environment of high culture for the select few, but at the same time reassuring the State that out of this would be produced visionary leaders that the country needed.

> But for the production of that limited body of men and women whose calling requires high talent, the University or its equivalent alone suffices. Moreover the University does more. For it is the indispensable portal to the career of the highest and most exceptionally trained type of citizen. Not knowledge, nor high quality, sought for the sake of some price to be obtained for them, but knowledge and quality for the sake of knowledge and quality are what are essential, and what the University must seek to produce.
>
> (Haldane 1912 p 71.)

The Values of the 'Liberal' University

Alongside the role of supplying manpower, then, liberal educationalists claimed that universities had a higher order mission of producing 'trained minds", graduate minds with developed rigorous thinking capacities. In effect the university was a civilising agent. As a general educative function, universities produced a continuous critique about ideas and people's place in society. As an important part of their independent role, they provided catalytic environments in which iconoclastic thinking was permissible.

In their pursuit of knowledge, most educationalists argued that universities should always be in the business of promoting beneficial things, either to the individual or to society at large. They had a responsibility to be conscious of the ongoing moral debate about the purposes of all human endeavour – what makes the world a better or a worse place. Indeed, they were part of a social context and should be contributing those values which beneficially help to shape that social context. Values which they claimed to uphold included those of human freedom, human dignity and democracy. In practice British universities represented an intellectual culture which was in theory accessible to a widening cross-section of society.

It was Dublin which proved to be the arena for one of the far-reaching statements on the importance of a liberal education. After the establishment of the Catholic University in 1854, Newman was appointed Rector. The backcloth to this new university had been the refusal of the Catholic Church to accept the validity of the three Queen's Colleges, at Belfast, Cork and Galway for Catholic education. Newman took up a stance against vocationalism and developed his ideas for a broader education of citizens in accordance with moral and intellectual values. Sceptical of the notion of narrow professional training, he emphasized the pursuit of knowledge in a disinterested fashion. In addition he stressed that collegiate identity, with students in residence on the campus, was vital to achieve these aims.

His aspiration was to produce graduates with civilized minds, through liberal education underpinned by theological studies. (J Coolahan 1981.) In fact the Catholic University ceased to exist in 1908 when it combined with the existing colleges in Cork and Galway to become the National University of Ireland. But Newman's 'Discourses on the Scope and Nature of University Education' became one of the great influential texts.

> When I speak of knowledge, I mean something intellectual, something which grasps what it perceives through the senses; something which takes a view of things; which sees more than the senses convey; which reasons upon what it sees, and while it sees; which invests it with an idea. It expresses itself, not in a mere enunciation, but by an enthymeme: it is the nature of science from the first and in this consists its dignity. The principle of real dignity in knowledge, its worth, its desirableness, considered irrespectively of its results, is this germ within it of a scientific or a philosophical process. This is how it comes to be an end in itself; this is why it admits of being called liberal. (J H Newman 1852/1965 p 92.)

The 'Red Bricks'

Durham and King's College London represented the end of the era of great Church of England foundations which carried with them an aura of almost mystical esteem:

> In 1832, three years after the foundation of the first London Colleges, the North of England gave birth to the first of its Universities, Durham. The connection of that University with the Church of England has given it, in the popular mind, a place apart, such as King's College, London, also an Anglican foundation, might have had but for its incorporation in a larger and an undenominational body. Its adoption in a modern form, of the collegiate system (Durham has eight colleges) and the association of two of its Chairs with canonries in Durham Cathedral enhance its prestige still further.
>
> (B Truscot 1951 p 24.)

It has been indicated that neither Oxford nor Cambridge were really geared to respond to the rapid changes brought about by the Industrial Revolution. Towards the end of the nineteenth and the beginning of the twentieth century, the phenomenon of the 'civic' or 'Red-Brick' university gained ground. Part of their rationale was that they would provide for students living within local catchment areas. Financed by endowments and municipal grants, they were intended to have a strong identification with geographical regions. In practice, many graduates of Oxford and Cambridge came to teach in the 'Red-Bricks' (so called literally because of the colour of the building materials). One such personage, who chose to write under the sibilant pseudonym of 'Truscot', commented on the reasoning of the benefactors who invested in these new institutions:

> They foresaw that, as the tide of prosperity in the country continued to rise, educational ideals and standards would rise with it and the four universities already in existence would soon be no longer sufficient for the national needs. They believed that a University established with noble, worthy and disinterested aims in the twentieth century would in time do as much for education as one that dated from the twelfth. They foresaw, again, that such a foundation could from the very first exercise a powerful moral and cultural influence upon the life of a large and rapidly growing community which was necessarily to a great extent preoccupied with material values.
>
> (B Truscot 1951 p 26.)

Right of Entry for Women

Accentuating the conclusion, however, that universities were far from egalitarian and accessible even by the end of the nineteenth century is the fact that women had no direct right of entry into higher education until the mid 1800s. Bedford College London was founded in 1849, to be followed by Cambridge's new colleges, Girton (1869) and Newnham (1871) and Oxford's initiatives in the form of Lady Margaret Hall (1879), Somerville (1879), St Hugh's (1886) and St Hilda's (1893).

The Great Post-War Expansion

It must also be remembered that there was no publicly funded system for student fees and maintenance until 1920, when state scholarships and county awards were initiated. Carswell reports that there were 51,000 full-time students attending British universities in 1935. This number had more than doubled to 113,000 students by 1961. (J Carswell 1985.)

In a prophetic statement, 'Truscot' suggested that a new era was about to dawn after the Second World War in which universities might have to re-examine some of their most enshrined principles:

We must be prepared for changes – and not only for the changes that we desire. If we proclaim aloud, as many of us are doing, that the new era brings with it new needs and new responsibilities for the nation, we must not forget that it also involves new obligations for ourselves. And chief among these is the obligation to examine any question afresh in the light of changed conditions – even principles which we had considered axiomatic and privileges to which we were so accustomed that we had to claim them for ourselves as rights. (B Truscot 1951 p 304.)

In the immediate post-war period, there were certainly considerable pressures to expand further the university system. As the provision and standards of secondary schooling improved, there was a substantial increase in student demand. In their attempts to compete with the rest of the world in accordance with the ground-rules of advanced capitalism, successive governments were increasingly aware of the need to extend and improve provisions for industrial and technological training. And there was an overall impression that much of the talent of the youth of the nation was not being properly tapped and channelled. Of immense significance in dictating the role of the modern university system was the Robbins Report which was published in 1963. One of its main recommendations was that courses in higher education should be made available and accessible to everyone who had the ability and attainment to participate in them, and of course expressed a wish to do so:

Two forces had brought about the expansion to which Robbins gave voice in Britain. One was the need, clearly perceived in the wake of the War, but never wholly satisfied, for graduates – above all for graduates in science and technology. The other was the ineluctable pressure for educational advance from one stage to the next, promoted by the concern (and in some cases the ambition) of parents, teachers and institutions. Both these forces were present in most countries, but in Britain the task of satisfying them was assumed in the years following the War, and by common consent, by the state. This was the unspoken axiom of the Robbins Report.

(J Carswell 1985 p 160.)

The Robbins Report advocated a diverse conglomeration of new universities, enhanced status for colleges of advanced technology and education, and development of 'sister' technological institutions. The latter development was later set in concrete by Anthony Crosland as the start of the 'binary system' whereby universities were artificially regarded as centres of pure studies and polytechnics took on the mantle of centres of applied studies.

Bureaucracy and Loss of Autonomy

According to Kedourie, the Robbins Report was to result in a massive increase in bureaucratisation within the university system. It also signified a much greater degree of centralized control by the state than had existed hitherto:

> There can be no doubt that this busy whirl in search of so-called facts and figures is the outcome of the hasty and injudicious expansion of the nineteen sixties – an expansion dictated by government, which government now finds itself unable or unwilling to fund in the manner to which its dependants had become accustomed. (E Kedourie 1988 p 21.)

The succeeding years saw a considerable heightening of tension in the debate as to whether universities could retain their integrity as intellectual cultures and at the same time contribute constructively to the trends towards vocational training. E P Thompson, who was teaching at Warwick University in the 1960s, tried to articulate the dilemma:

> Is it inevitable that the university will be reduced to the function of providing with increasingly authoritarian efficiency, pre-packed intellectual commodities which meet the requirements of management?

> Or can we by our efforts transform it into a centre of free discussion and action, tolerating and even encouraging subversive thought and activity, for a dynamic renewal of the whole society within which it operates?
>
> (E P Thompson 1970 p 166.)

There was widespread concern that many of the positive features represented by universities were now coming under serious threat. The autonomy represented in freedom of choice of courses to be taught, research to be undertaken, methods employed in promoting learning, was believed to be as important and beneficial to surrounding society as it was to the universities themselves. Kedourie mourned the loss of what he maintained was a relationship between academic staff and prospective employers of graduates that was more in tune with public interests:

> Better suited, because their judgement whether to teach this subject or not, in this or that manner, or to pursue this or that enquiry, or that this university or department was better than that one – such judgements were informed judgements arising out of a living, intimate and lifelong engagement with the matter in hand. These issues did not issue from the desire – benevolent as it may be – to execute social justice, or in pursuit of the illusion that universities can be made into instruments of social engineering.
>
> (E Kedourie 1988 p 18.)

Unfortunately the perceptions of university students by the general public in the 1960s and 1970s were far removed from visions of potentially useful citizens. Students came to be regarded as "disruptive, work-shy, and, above all, dangerously politicized." (M Warnock 1988 p 137.)

Identity Crisis

In assessing the pressures for change in higher education, it is imperative to take account of the economic context of Britain since the 1960s. There is a rampant mythology that depicts the 1960s as optimistic, buoyant and full of vitality. In reality there were many underlying social problems, not least the continuation of poverty and structural inequalities, which could arguably reduce any such claims to misplaced hyperbole. Nonetheless there was undoubtedly a palpable impact on Britain in the early 1970s when the world oil price instability erupted and the economy suffered a series of inflationary crises. Inevitably the primary purposes of higher education had to come under examination. Was the process of education in university fundamentally and exclusively concerned with the individual self-development and fulfilment of potential of the student? Or did universities share with other societal institutions a responsibility to serve the needs of the economy, and prepare students more specifically to take their places as trained key workers in the occupational structure?

> The extended economic recession of the 1970s and 1980s, and the accompanying high levels of unemployment and growing disenchantment with education, have brought with them renewed attempts by pressure groups and policy-makers to strengthen the links between education and the economy. It is claimed that schools and colleges should serve the needs of industry and commerce more directly and effectively.
>
> (Pollard, Purvis and Walford 1988 p 4.)

The Political Stencil

It was the task of the Conservative Government to articulate its ideological position in relation to the future of the universities in its White Paper 'Higher Education – Meeting the Challenge' (CM 114 1987). The bricks of its new educational edifice were plain to see. University funding was to be placed in the hands of a new University Funding Council which would bring the sixty year existence of the University Grants Committee to an end. There were to be substantial increases in student numbers, and efforts were to be made to extend age group participation. 'Pick up' courses were to be introduced, self-financing and paid for by employers, in order to provide continuing professional training and updating for employees.

In future, the Government would provide funding for the universities through a system of 'contracts'. Explicitly it was stated that universities were expected to serve the economy effectively and that preferential support would be given to science, engineering and business-related social sciences courses. Furthermore research funding would be consciously aimed at specific areas which indicated good possibilities for commercial exploitation. The importance of efficiency within the universities was emphasized and it was announced that management practices would literally be monitored in the future through the use of 'performance indicators'. These measurement devices were further elaborated in the Jarratt Report of 1985 which also outlined the desired hierarchical structures which would maximize efficiency and effectiveness. An unambiguous downward transmission model of management, it centred around a fundamental change in the role of Vice Chancellors who were to take on active executive responsibilities. As a further reinforcement of the vocational education emphasis, the Training Commission was empowered to distribute finance to widen a scheme entitled 'Enterprise in Higher Education'. Funding would be provided for work experience placements, or student projects aimed at developing students' managerial and business skills.

Enterprise Culture

Clearly, the universities had been declared to be an integral part of 'the enterprise culture'. Alongside the government's unremitting scaling down of the importance of the public sector in the national economy, universities would have to be more self-reliant and become in effect private profit-seeking enterprises under centralized control and direction. They would have to learn to sell their wares giving as high a quality as possible as cheaply as possible to outside bidders among whom would be the government itself.

Allen saw these developments as the inevitable result of disillusionment and inflated optimism about the benefits of higher education:

> It has to be remembered that by 1981 public opinion had changed, and not only as a result of the student unrest. Higher education had been portrayed by the Robbins Report and by politicians of the 1960s as a solution to many social ills and needs: but by 1981 it could be agreed that the system had failed to deliver, and the atmosphere was right for money to be saved.

(M Allen 1988 p 47.)

Relationship with the State

In tracing the history of the administration of British universities, Carswell argues that, while universities have always been self-governing institutions with their own incomes and property, it is fallacious to assert that they did not form part of the state.

He suggests that what has really happened is a progression from the relatively small world of universities at the beginning of the century with informal social links with government to a modern and more complex set of social and economic relationships:

> The universities of fifty years ago were very closely integrated with the state as it then was, but in a quite different way, and they formed just as indispensable part of the framework of national institutions as they do now. The links, however, were personal and social, not bureaucratic or formal. The universities and the machinery of Government in both its political and official aspects formed a kind of continuum, in which only the sketchiest of formality was either expected or required to maintain necessary relationships. This was enormously assisted by the small size of the university world and by its concentration in a comparatively few powerful centres. An obscure and confidential committee was all that was required to transfer the marginal – but essential – Exchequer publicly to the institutions in a decorous and impartial way. (J Carswell 1985 p 159.)

This point was underlined concisely and clearly by the former Minister for Education himself when he declared that:

> The structures appropriate to higher education with 3 per cent participation, or even 13 per cent participation, simply cannot be sustained when participation rises to 30 per cent. (K Baker 1989.)

Loss of Tenure

Accompanying the ideological harnessing of the universities in the drive towards more economic growth and affluence, there has been anxiety bordering on dismay among educationalists in the face of potential threats to academic freedom of expression. When the Education Reform Act eventually appeared in 1988, the Government appeared to have retreated to an extent on this issue. However the tangible evidence of its determination to bring universities into line with other social institutions was present, in that 'tenure' or the holding of an academic position for life, was abolished. In practice it had always been possible to dismiss university staff for carefully defined reasons, but now in reality new academic staff or those promoted or transferred no longer have the guarantee of a secure post. In the growing atmosphere of alienated paranoia, there is the obvious concern that, in future, certain academic posts which lose credibility in the struggle to be self-financing (and inevitably some Humanities and Social Sciences fields appear most vulnerable), will be frozen or removed from the staffing establishment with the result that academic staff could be declared redundant.

The Utilitarian Model

In a vigorous pronouncement of the place of higher education within modern conservative dogma, the Minister of Education left nothing to the imagination; describing the implementation of his policies as:

> movement towards mass higher education accompanied by greater institutional differentiation and diversification in a market-led and multi-funded setting.   (K Baker 1989.)

At the same time, he attempted to reassure that the basic tenets of university education can and will be preserved, and are compatible with modern needs to produce highly trained workers for the labour force:

> In my view, the pursuit of knowledge as an object of interest in and for itself remains the cornerstone of the whole higher education edifice. But knowledge for its own sake is not and has never been the only value of importance in higher education. Alongside the disinterested pursuit of knowledge, feeding off it and also vitalizing it, 'vocationalism' has always had its place in education – which has always performed an important service function.   (K Baker 1989.)

In apparent if reluctant admiration of this lucidity of vision, Kedourie described the Government's interventionist strategy as:

> a tough-minded, no-nonsense crusade for utility as the alpha and omega of university education.   (E Kedourie 1988 p 10.)

However he fears that the future of universities as a source of great riches is going to be in great doubt in the face of procedures which attempt to quantify and rate practices according to their utilitarian value:

> The great value of Aladdin's Cave is that its riches are wholly unexpected and uncovenanted. The moment a licensed valuer is sent to make a survey according to ruling market prices, the charm is broken, gold turns to lead, diamonds to glass.   (E Kedourie 1988 p 6).

The Ecological Model

Obviously reeling under the welter of market place terminology which has been injected into higher education vocabulary, Bassey indicates that students have become 'consumers' or 'customers'; that universities are being required to address "the challenge of employment in tomorrow's world"; and that there is apparently a race against time to match standards which are rising in "competitor countries" (M Bassey 1987). He has coined the term 'wealthism' to try to incorporate all these new values which are being transmitted through the government:

> Wealthism is an ideology – meaning a coherent set of beliefs held fervently by a group of people – which sees the creation of wealth as the prime function of the active members of society. If you have wealth you can feed, protect and provide shelter for your family. With wealth you can buy goods and property and entertainment; with more wealth you can buy better goods and property and entertainment. If you have sufficient wealth you can buy medical treatment and buy education for your children. The more wealth you have, the greater the opportunity for satisfaction. To the wealthist, happiness is in the shape of a pound sign. (M Bassey 1987 p 4.)

He proceeds to argue that the economic growth model is misplaced because there is evidence that Western European countries and perhaps even the United States are in sight of social and economic limitations to growth. With the present increases in world population, the continuing drive towards greater industrialization, food production, pollution and the general depletion of resources, the capacity for production will be drastically reduced within another hundred years. This vulnerable and precarious plight affecting all human beings should, he asserts, be the central concern of the educational system. The development of strategies to establish ecological as well as economic stability that could be sustained should be regarded as the paramount social issue of our times. Concerted efforts should be made to achieve a form of global equilibrium whereby the essential living needs of all human beings can be met and everyone can be given the genuine opportunity to identify and develop their potential talents whatever form they take.

This is an articulate renunciation of the current political philosophy which encourages greed and self-advancement in a free-floating market economy and which appears to deny the existence of power imbalances and inequalities among the citizens of the state. Bassey seeks to substitute mutual aid in the common interest in place of individual aggrandisement at whatever expense and issues words of caution about the ways in which higher education is being expected to collude with such a negative ideology.

Social Injustice

The theme of persisting inequalities is taken up by Shipman who argues that the expansionism of the universities failed to make any real inroads into the social injustices in British society. And while there is a need for social criticism, research and scholarship in our society, this can be accomplished by a university system which is smaller in size and therefore less demanding on national resources:

> When resources were scarce it was difficult to defend the universities and higher education against cuts. The expansion had not visibly increased

social justice or even educational opportunity and the economy declined as universities expanded. Those who went to university found that a degree was no longer a ticket to high-status employment or even a mark of prestige.

The economy, the civil service, the schools, the welfare services and the professions all require an intake of well-qualified entrants. A democracy is kept on its toes by social scientists. Life is enriched through scholarship in the arts. Research is increasingly the prerequisite of high technology industry. Scholarship is an end in itself. But a very small university sector could provide the scholarship, the research and the social criticism. In practice most activity in higher education is concerned with the quality of life of those involved, not investment in industry or criticism of social arrangements. It is a pleasant three or more years for students and a rewarding life for staff. The injustice is that these rewards go to such a limited range of the population and not necessarily to all the most talented. But for all, the return from the investment fell as supply outstripped demand in the market for graduate employment.   (M Shipman 1984 p 168.)

Social Contract

Ultimately, however, Carswell had his finger on the modern pulse most sensitively when he suggested that there can be a consensual bond between universities and the nation at large without insisting on some form of strait-jacketed uniformity. He maintained that, in spite of esoteric image cultivated not only in critiques of university life but in the behavioural styles adopted by many academics, it is an illusion to regard universities as apart from 'the workaday world'. They are subject to the same generic necessities in that they have to compete for funds, to generate interest in student applicants, and to develop good reputations for scholarship. If the flexible climate is permitted that enables universities to garner these rewards, it is pointless to exert pressure on them for 'responsiveness' and 'relevance'. They are already highly alert to the currents of ordinary life that surround them, and indeed, by dint of their own needs for survival, reflect these societal currents in manifold ways themselves:

> Subject to certain lags as opinion changes course, a nation will get what it needs from its universities if funds, students and reputation are allowed them.   (J Carswell 1985 p 167).

Focus on the Client

Doidge and Whitechurch, reflecting on the Jarratt Report, note that this caused universities to develop their structure, strategies and systems – the 'Hard S's'. To meet the challenge of the 1990s, to do more with less, they suggest that higher education has to concentrate on the 'soft S's', that is staff, style, skills and shared values. Advocating a 'Total Quality management' approach, they argue that every effort should be made to develop understanding of the people with whom they interact, the students, the research contractors, or the local community. Actual survival may depend on it!

> We are faced with a major challenge in an increasingly competitive world and are in competition for resources and customers. We need help from whatever source to enable us to survive and to be successful, and increasingly higher education is being judged on its quality in terms of what it actually delivers in teaching, research and in its services.
>
> (Doidge and Whitechurch p 5 1993.)

Competition and Collaboration

During the year of 1992, as a result of the Further and Higher Education Act, there was a very substantial enlargement of the British university system when most of the former polytechnics adopted university titles. At the same time, the responsibility for funding of the Higher Education section was assumed by new Higher Education Funding Councils for England, Wales and Scotland. Appropriately, a meeting took place in November 1992 at UMIST of the Corporate Planning Forum of the Conference of University Administrators (now the Association of University Administrators, having since merged with the association of their polytechnic colleagues). In the ensuing discussions, useful definitions emerged of the areas of tension in terms of competition and collaboration between universities in the present economic climate. Clearly there would be competition in seeking student life-blood, and in pursuing external funding for research and other activities. If efficiency gains and a clearer focus on objectives resulted, so much the better. However it was felt that the notion of free-market competition was rather inappropriate and unreal when applied to the planning and administration of the Higher Education system. A more managed approach was desirable, in which institutional sharing could be encouraged, particularly when complementary interests would be strengthened. Especially at local or regional level, benefits could ensue for students and staff if running costs and talents could be shared. Inter-institutional areas of likely co-operation were identified as: staff resources for teaching; staff resources for research; the uses of expensive equipment; staff development; information technology; physical resources such as sports and teaching facilities; and joint approaches to meet demands arising from the introduction of third semesters. (Jones (ed) Corporate Planning Forum, CUA 1992.)

Value-Added

In the course of this book, it will be argued that there is an explicit responsibility on the part of higher education to demonstrate to wider society what benefits will accrue both to social groupings and to individual students if they choose to make use of the intellectual culture offered within universities. With regard to individual students, it will be demonstrated that educational institutions must provide the stimulus required for the personal development of students in a holistic sense, incorporating not just intellectual growth, but social, emotional and cultural development as well. Only by addressing the issue of higher learning in an imaginative and comprehensive manner, will the universities be able to rise to the challenge currently being mounted and affirm a valid role for themselves as the twentieth century comes to a close.

Chapter Two

The Function of Modern Higher Education

In the previous narrative history, it was illustrated that there were differentiated stages of University development. These can be summarized as: the 'medieval' university, the 'liberal' university and the 'welfare state' university. The medieval university looked to the supreme authority of religion and eventually offered an undiluted elitist educational experience, from which most of its students could expect to proceed to the highest professions in the social structure. From the mid 1800s, the liberal university ethos emerged, with its basis in cognitive and humanist values, and an allegiance to the authority of science and intellectual rigour. After the second world war, heralded by the Robbins Report, the 'welfare state' universities mushroomed, absorbing many of the liberal values but geared more instrumentally to serve the interests of the state and the economy. Parallel to this growth, polytechnics expanded rapidly in Britain, offering a wide range of applied technological and vocational courses. As a result of the Further and Higher Education Act of 1992, these institutions, with breathtaking unanimity, grasped the opportunity to adopt university titles, so marking the end of the 'binary line' in British higher education. The impact of the influx of 'new' universities on the numbers of registered students in 1992–3 has been dramatic:

'Old' universities	357,000	full-time
	11,000	part-time
'New' universities	479,000	full-time
	267,000	part-time

(Source: Department of Education, London, May 1993.)

Many of these students are taking up technological or middle management positions within the British industrial state.

Scott identified how these historical trends carried with them significant implications for both the status of the intellectual culture of the liberal university and the power relations between universities and wider society.

That quality of standing slightly apart from Society, of transcendence in both time and place of parochial intellectualoid preoccupations in the cause of a universal intellectual tradition which had been an important feature of the liberal university, was very much eroded in the 30 years of explosive university growth after 1945. Universities became almost entirely instrumental institutions losing their semi-spiritual quality. More and more they were seen as institutions that could make a direct and powerful contribution to the acceleration of economic growth or the promotion of social justice, not simply through the students they educated or the academic knowledge they discovered and elaborated but in quite immediate and specific ways. Knowledge itself was seen as the primary product of higher education, not students. Everyone and everything was in a hurry; so it seemed natural to try to make advances in science (social and human as well as natural) immediately and directly useful to society through the route of technology, rather than to allow them to feed slowly and indirectly into society through the medium of pedagogy.

...knowledge became more subservient to power. (P Scott 1984 p 54.)

Bearing in mind this transition, the main thrust of this book is not only to celebrate and reassert the bedrock academic values associated with liberal universities, but to argue vigorously that the maintenance of these values in the protected world of higher education is crucial for democratic society. Furthermore it is postulated that it is vital for the more technological universities born into the welfare state to allow their operating principles to be imbued with liberal values in order to retain their academic integrity and focus on a clear sense of purpose.

Pursuit of Knowledge

Consequently, at this time of great challenge when the purpose of higher education is being closely scrutinized, it is essential to reflect on and adhere to these inviolable principles which, it will be argued, validate the very existence of universities. Derived from the Latin 'universitas', the literal and most acceptable modern meaning of a university is a corporately organized corporation, society or community. The traditional liberal definition of the function of a university is this corporately organized devotion to a search after knowledge "for the sake of its intrinsic value." (B Truscot 1951 p 65). Interestingly, the Robbins Report, in the midst of its recommendations for the massive expansion of higher education, embraced wholeheartedly these core principles:

...the search for truth is an essential function of institutions of higher education and the process of education is itself most vital when it partakes of the nature of discovery. It would be untrue to suggest that the advancement of knowledge has been or ever will be wholly dependent on universities and other institutions of higher education. But the world, not higher education alone, will suffer if ever they cease to regard it as one of their main functions.

(Robbins Report Vol 1 (1963) p 7.)

Allen succinctly summarizes the three basic missions of higher education to transmit, to extend and to apply knowledge (M Allen 1988). While this does accurately reflect the tasks of the academic staff, it is perhaps too narrow in that it does not allow for the interactive process between the tutors and the students. In addition to these three central 'missions', academic tutors should also be prepared to encourage incoming students to reorganize and value the knowledge base which they already possess, and indeed the tutors should be sufficiently open to learn from their students. Referring again to Latin derivatives, the word 'education' is derived from either 'educare' – to bring up or to rear – or 'educere' – to lead forth. The latter definition with its active emphasis is preferred.

While retaining the concept of the corporately organized academic institution, it is important to emphasize that the process of learning does not as a result have to be confined to one physical building or campus. The presence of the university in any region can cover a wide geographical area, with the possibility of multiple 'out-centres' and different modes of study if the student cannot or prefers not to engage in full-time day attendance.

An essential and integrated element in the learning process is that of research. Universities pursue research of two distinguishable varieties. 'Pure' research is the pursuit of knowledge for its own sake. 'Applied' research is directed at the resolution of certain specified problems which are usually located in an industrial or commercial context. In either case rigorous academic methodology is applied whether the aim is scholarly investigation; appreciation; creative and textual criticism; reinterpretation; or critical treatment of contemporary thought. The process of research is not complete, however, unless the initiator has committed the work to the form of a written treatise and offered the findings to other researchers for replication or refutation.

> The act is completed only with diffusion; and although in the most literal
> sense a certain amount of diffusion can be accomplished viva voce, in
> lectures and in seminars there is no permanence about this.
>
> (B Truscot 1951 p 337.)

Higher Education as a Socializing Agent
People who enter higher education are exposed to other ways of thinking, other points of view. They interact with fellow students as well as staff. This could be

said to be a sort of accidental socialisation, to be distinguished from indoctrination or conditioning. A very clear set of ideas is reproduced in a fairly harmonious way; and universities may inculcate those harmonious values or ideas in their students. As a result the bulk of students probably emerge from higher education with a reinforced sense of values which are central to the society in which they will continue to live and work. Yet at the same time academic institutions in themselves retain a certain kind of pluralism in which dissident ideas are promulgated, both at the level of staff and at the level of students. So universities do socialize students but could not be labelled as some sinister reflection of external social control mechanisms. They socialize the students into their intellectual cultures in a manner which should not be authoritarian. Indeed through encouraging interaction with the wider community, the institution can exert a healthy energizing influence which is to the mutual benefit of the college, the students and the community. However, far from indoctrination and unquestioning collusion, the institution should represent the most iconoclastic element in the educational system. This is the feature which sets is most vividly apart from primary and secondary levels of education. Schools on the whole tend to be concerned with transmitting traditional values, whereas universities are more orientated towards challenging and examining afresh all ideas. Renewal, revision, enquiry and challenge should be key words in their vocabulary. Third level academic institutions also provide the opportunity for people to learn to live and work together at a time when most students are coming to the end of adolescence and are still very much in the process of developing personal identities. Increasingly very different personalities from a wide range of backgrounds meet for the first time on equal terms. Higher education gives them the opportunity to learn to understand themselves and how to interact with other people in addition to the intellectual stimulation of academic study.

Accountability to Society

Higher education is a public service and consequently all universities should overtly state their social purposes and be required to be accountable to the wider society. Third level education has a tremendous contribution to make to the 'health' of society, alongside the other services of the welfare state. And since higher education institutions in spite of more flexible access and admissions criteria, are still dealing with the potential leaders of our society, they must be answerable for their actions. This must not be taken to mean that academic establishments need only be accountable to a certain 'fraction' of society. Under the present British electoral system, to be accountable to a political entity that claims to be representative of society, in other words a current government, would in fact mean allegiance to a political dogma which only commands 40% of the popular vote! Accountability must be to the whole society, including those who are most powerless within it.

> ... human societies are and probably always will be politically split. In virtue of values that lie at its very foundation, the university is inevitably involved in these splits in so far as these values are at stake. In relation to the conflict between the idea of impartial thinking and the idea that we cannot think except in accordance with the interest of a race or a class, it is not neutral; nor is it neutral in the conflict between those who do and those who do not believe that tolerance is better than police control over teaching.

> It follows that the idea of the university is not violated when the university is actively engaged in issues directly bound up with its functioning according to its own basic principles; that the university is in duty bound to react in all cases where such issues as freedom of teaching, freedom of research, freedom of discussion, opposition to compulsory indoctrination etc become the target of political conflict.

> (L Kolakowski/A Montefiore 1975 p 79.)

The extent of accountability is debatable at present as some academic institutions retain elitist positions which are rooted in their histories. In contrast there are some aspects of academic self-government which are quite democratic collegiate structures. Of fundamental importance in validating their future roles is a clear commitment by universities through democratized decision-making procedures to engage the public directly in their affairs and to open up for examination both their strength and their weaknesses.

Regional Identification

There is a case for greater accountability to democratic government, preferably on a localized regional basis, which could surmount the problem of government social control being exercised on the basis of a minority vote. It is much more coherent to develop an accountability to the locality in which the university is sited. 'Truscot' developed a similar rationale nearly forty years ago in order to promote colourful and imaginative creativity as opposed to monochrome imitation.

> Even in a country no larger than our own it is well known that regional characteristics and interest should be preserved, and it is to be hoped that determined resistance will meet the efforts made from time to time to supplant them all by a drab national conformity. Our universities, well placed as they are, form excellent centres for regional development.

> (B Truscot 1951 p 356.)

It should be a duty of all academic staff to engage in studies, reflecting their specialist fields, into the special problems or issues of the particular region in which the college is located. Departments or Faculties should come to represent centres of information and ideas on their respective areas of interest, be it history, dialect, geology, social policy, environmental science, social anthropology, town planning. Local citizens should have access to the academic staff for help and guidance ranging from political, social, international matters to philosophical and moral issues. The guidance should be in order to inculcate good habits of inquiry into such concerns, how to consider and weigh evidence in favour or antagonistic to certain propositions.

In a sense, the university could regard all citizens as constituents of the region. They would have automatic right of entry onto the campus to savour and enjoy the same stimulation to which the full-time student has access. Thus the clubs and societies should have community 'associate' membership; the library reading rooms should have special visitor privileges; there should be open access to the theatrical events, musical concerts, art exhibitions, film evenings, sport and leisure pursuits. Reciprocally the academic staff should offer their services to the local radio and television stations as a means of communicating ideas en masse or commenting on important topics of the day.

'Truscot' advocated that local 'correspondents' could be appointed to liaise with the 'extension society', keeping interest in academic pursuits alive and stimulating people to ask for more participation. (B Truscot 1951). It is appreciated that many universities already engage in extensive outreach activities in local communities. What is being emphasized here is that the third level institution should take a definitive lead from local citizens about their own needs and desires, as opposed to the more directive approach of setting up courses which would be "good for them". In addition to the accepted practice of camping out in local colleges or community centres, there is an argument that the higher education establishment should establish a series of 'Academic Houses' in key positions within a region who would serve as public meeting places. This would represent a healthy breaking down of the elitist notion that the citizen must make the effort to travel to and cross the mystical boundary of the campus as some sort of sacrosanct entity.

Having said that, there is however also a case for opening up the facilities such as student residences on a more imaginative basis when possible. One example would be the promotion of out-of-term summer schools under the auspices of local history groups, language societies, environmental organizations, WEAs, women's groups, short courses on information technology. The essential motivation behind such initiatives would always have to be the genuine desire to demystify the process of higher education and to make the campus a welcoming environment.

The Significance of the Charter

It is essential that the role of the universities in society is protected through their Charters. The Charter is the means by which the university publicly pronounces its set of guiding principles or ideals and by which it will test all its actions. These values underpin the untrammelled pursuit of knowledge and consequently universities must be protected from having to endorse the dominant party political lines, traditional ways of thinking, or fashionable modes of thought. Being too answerable to the prevailing government of the day might endanger the necessary function of the university in challenging whatever is currently the ambient philosophy. Thus there must be a clear degree of independence from the wider society. The balance is between independent autonomy and finding a way of showing society that the money it invests in universities in research and in the education and training of its students is in fact cost effective. Ultimately there has to be an accountability in the sense that universities must show that they are giving value for money spent. The value for money spent is not easy to quantify – for instance the encouragement of creativity or pushing back the frontiers of knowledge through fundamental research initiatives are not always easily open to measurement. However an attempt will be made later in this book to demonstrate that qualitative measurement may be possible. There is an obligation to explore such routes and try to perfect instruments of measurement in order to demonstrate publicly the unique strengths within the university system.

Perhaps the real question is to what extent should universities be accountable? They need sufficient autonomy to be able to draw up the lines for their own progressive development. Thus instead of too directive and unilateral an accountability, it should be more the case of an interactive relationship between universities and wider society. Universities should reflect and respond to the needs and changes in society; at the same time university staff can continually feed back ideas and concepts into society through various means. In turn society should be prepared to absorb, integrate and if appropriate adjust to these ideas and perspectives. This form of dynamic mutualism would ensure that universities would retain their freshness and vigour and preserve their important critical edge, while being answerable for their actions.

The Ultimate Value of Higher Education

As already indicated, universities are complex organizations with their own historical inheritances and consequently it is important not to appear to impose too simplistic a model. However, there are ultimate values about which there is a strong consensus within academic institutions and which transcend the raw economic needs to keep functioning and survive in hard times! Basically in Britain these consist of a set of democratic liberal values which may be denigrated by others as being irrelevant to current social problems and social needs, but actually offer a coherent sense of direction for the talents and energies of staff and students, whatever fields of study they may be undertaking. Within the liberal ideal type ethos, the primary value is pursuit of truth and eternal vigilance in identifying illogical or invalid ways of thinking in practice that blur the perception of truth. Institutions of higher education in effect represent tolerance, giving an audience to a wide variety of views however currently unfashionable they might be, however abhorrent to the listener. They have to and will defend the necessity for public proclamation of any views and provide the forum for public examination of these views. Thus tolerance and openness to examination are important kinds of values in higher education. Acutely central and essential to the proper functioning of universities are independence of thought and expression; freedom to develop ideas and express opinions; and freedom of access to information. This latter value is particularly significant in that much information for instance in relation to research is in the hands of outside systems and the degree of access to that information is variable.

In essence, universities represent bastions for democratic humanitarianism; they recognize the central importance of individual human dignity and worth; they favour and promote social justice. A high emphasis is placed on learning for its own sake. Many of the ideas promoted are about human beings living with one another harmoniously and tolerantly without violence. Arguably institutions of higher education in defending these values if needs be to their last dying breath, represent solid and dependable cornerstones of any truly democratic society. Even more significantly, they will always be the arch critics of any regime which aims to subvert democratic values in pursuit of totalitarian aims.

The Promotion of Social Change

Universities produce new information, new analyses of social problems and social issues, new ideas; and they disseminate these ideas into the wider world. Thus this must inevitably lead to social change however gradual and however immeasurable. Notwithstanding the audience for these new ideas tends to be extraordinarily limited. The world of industry is a clear recipient of many higher education initiatives; a relatively narrow set of academic journals and books also become the recipients of ideas that are being generated. So while it is potentially a very powerful agent, a university has a very restricted capacity because of its limited audience. Nonetheless the capacity of the academic institution to effect change indirectly and non-judgementally remains a reality. Having said that, fundamental social change in society has to be fought for and implemented through mass democratic means. Universities are not really part of mass democratic structures and are not really political institutions. Where they have a valid role is in breathing life into mass democracy by showing what alternatives are possible given certain problems and given certain circumstances. So they are about promoting ideas, indicating different possibilities, and feeding these into the democratic process. It should be emphasized at the same time that everything academic institutions do, as with the rest of society, is value-laden. Work by staff, students, research assistants, automatically and inevitably reflects political or value positions, so third level colleges cannot pretend to contribute to wider policy in any value-free way. Therefore even in the process of disseminating ideas and weighing up alternatives, the work of the authors reflects particular stances. This being so, it is crucial that universities exercise tolerance in terms of making sure that within their own collegiate bodies, they have a range of political opinion. Academic democracy can be enlivened and refreshed through a range of ideas; these ideas are then made available to wider society, perhaps leading to social change through democratic means. The beauty about the generation of new ideas by higher education institutions is that they are not constrained by dominant political ideology and economic structures. An analysis can show in a Utopian sense what could be possible given social change in certain directions.

In summary, then, institutions of higher education do not have any kind of mandate to promote social change. Their values are only defensible as part of an organization concerned simply with the examination of arguments, points of view, and displaying the strengths or crudities of such arguments. The other democratic elements in society who do have political mandates take what they can from the evidence that emanates from higher education sources. Perhaps decisions are then made politically by others from the point of view of benign social engineering. But it is not the business of the universities to spell out the social implications and the political imperatives of the knowledge and arguments that originate within their portals.

The vital nature of this potential contribution to the social change process is however exemplified in the current economic debate in Britain. The emergence of the Conservative economic policy wherein the market place is the regulator and policies are mounted to monitor all economic behaviour has been a feature of the last fourteen years of political life in Britain. Universities have a valid role in continually reviewing and debating the effectiveness of these policies. The strengths and weaknesses of the economic model and its effectiveness should be presented as information from the academic sector to the wider society so that every five years, at general elections, the electorate can make an informed choice.

This is quite distinct from third level institutions attempting to claim infallibility or prescribe what is desirable and what is not desirable for society. To identify a main direction in which change should be pursued would run the risk of indulgence in academic totalitarianism. On the other hand, scholarly research actually does push back the frontiers of knowledge and this inevitably makes a contribution to change. For instance, there is clear evidence of such positive changes in the world of medicine, environmentalism and information technology. Universities should limit their roles to articulating the different options which are available in terms of change and the probable predictable consequences arising from these options. In any case the views of academia as to what is good for society may not be what society in general would accept. Academic establishments represent a particular stratification of the population and inevitably have different ideas, choices and views from society in general. They should not attempt to foist these on society any more than public representatives should insist on acceptance of their own pronouncements by the academic world. Indeed, it is salutary to reflect on the fact that academics in their life-styles and work patterns possibly do not fully know what the external world of work is really like and in fact are a group of very privileged people. This fact is vividly illustrated by David Lodge in the fictional form of a university lecturer engaged in an industrial exchange programme:

> It was the most terrible place she had ever been in her life. To say that to herself restored the original meaning of the word 'terrible': it provoked terror, even a kind of awe. To think of being that man, wrestling with the heavy awkward lumps of metal in that maelstrom of heat, dust and stench, deafened by the unspeakable noise of the vibrating grid, working like that for hour after hour, day after day... (D Lodge 1988 p 90.)

Higher Education and Cultural Awareness
According to Dario Fo:

> Economic change is not enough. Without culture we cannot change the world. (D Fo 1983 p 32.)

He argues that culture in its broadest sense has an essential part to play in reinforcing the collective experience. It is postulated in this book that higher education must contribute towards a positive cultural climate which can only grow out of a collective consciousness and which recognizes and does not seek to repress social diversity. To help achieve a more positive form of cultural enrichment in society, which would enhance the lives of all citizens, universities have a major role to play alongside other social institutions. Western countries are experiencing ideological turmoil, the crisis of hegemony of the bourgeoisie manifesting itself as a crisis within individual subjectivities. Even in Sweden, which has been vaunted as the epitome of civilized social policy, concern is now being expressed about the degree of alienation, distance, stigmatization being experienced by young people. These represent all the problems of a crisis of motivation. To provide a substantial alternative, intervention is necessary into the sorts of existence which have been atomising, fragmenting, driving people back into their homes and impoverishing social relationships. If these positive interventions are to be achieved, it is important not to reinforce old dichotomies. In particular universities must move away from the socially divisive notion that they represent some form of 'high culture', an essentially elitist notion which says that only those who can aspire to join the select campus society can enjoy the benefits. Without detracting in any way from the potential joys of listening to classical music, or attending an art exhibition, these tend to be viewed as rather restrictive bourgeois activities and only form part of a much wider spectrum that one might term 'cultural enrichment'.

It is not possible or appropriate to predict in advance the exact configuration of future structures, their model of operation and detailed content of the ideological transformations that could be achieved. In accordance with McLennan, it is important to adopt a position of realism in methodology whereby every kind of proposition is held conditionally. A dialogical process by its very nature can have no predetermined ends (G McLennan 1981). However it is possible to outline a set of operational principles that can be generated in order to help guide the process towards greater cultural enrichment and indicate some of the ways in which institutions of higher education might participate in this process.

Potentially cultural enrichment has to reflect a balance between a developed sense of collective effort and a recognition of the potential values of social diversity as opposed to a repressive conformity. If simultaneous collectivity and diversity can be presented as the constituents of social life, their potential for cultural enrichment is not always clearly visible, but the capacity for positive development will be there by virtue of the essence of social relationships. While this collectivity and diversity will generate both positive and negative outcomes, its existence is crucial to new modes of thinking and coexisting. The thrust will not consist purely of a toleration of diversity. There will be an encouragement of belief in the inherent potential for enrichment for its own sake – the positive alternatives to the current life of fatalism and passivity that confronts many citizens.

When one tries to visualize the potential within a campus for cultural responses to modernism, the possibilities are immense. The accumulation of rich resources that results from the combined efforts of students, staff and members of the surrounding community offer a potent admixture of talent, energy and creativity.

This might take the form of musical evenings where the ancient folk traditions of a region can come face to face with modern musical interpretations. In the arena of drama, the theatre studies programme might range from Restoration Comedies to current community group projects in which all the humour and contradictions of modern working class family life are depicted. The evening art classes might build in an appreciation of the Pre-Raphaelites and at the same time encourage the participants to enjoy and place in social context the primitive but highly expressive art which abounds in many regions of the country and has not necessarily been tutored in any formal technique.

This concept of cultural enrichment is a far cry from the exclusive and highly objectionable notion that citizens can only aspire to culture if they have the wealth to purchase it. This latter sterile model really represents the mercenary acquisition of other people's talents, the treatment of the arts as assets or commodities, not to be enjoyed but to be preserved for the purposes of social prestige or resaleable value. In contrast the cultural enrichment which higher education should reinforce has to do with the fostering of the belief that all human beings can not only enjoy but personally participate in the creation of their own culture. Imagination can be transcribed by anyone into the form of poetry. Art can take on a beauty of form and shape which is literally in the eye of the beholder. Experimentation in music individually and collectively can be a very demonstrable reflection of the life, hopes, fears and humour of a local community. Instead of the greedy acquisition and exclusive possession of bits of the surrounding world, academic institutions should be encouraging all citizens to participate fully in the creation of their own culture and the transformation of their own worlds. This is not to say that the campus becomes a Mecca to which the mere citizen comes to bow in worshipful reverence.

Rather the campus should be an open forum, a catalytic agent which helps transform the talents, resources and energies of the surrounding community into new rich forms which all can enjoy.

Chapter Three

Access to Higher Education

While acknowledging the political importance of higher education producing more graduates in order to meet the perceived challenge of international competition, the Robbins Report is also notable for its profound commitment to the principle of equality of opportunity to pursue one's personal development in a much wider sense:

> Throughout our Report we have assumed as an axiom that courses of higher education should be available for all those who are qualified by ability and attainment and who wish to do so.
>
> If challenged, however, we would vindicate it on two grounds. First, conceiving education as a means, we do not believe that modern societies can achieve their aims of economic growth and higher cultural standards without making the most of the talents of their citizens. This is obviously necessary if we are to compete with other highly developed countries in an era of rapid technological and social advance. But, even if there were not the spur of international standards, it would still be true that to realise the aspirations of a modern community as regards both wealth and culture, a fully educated population is necessary.
>
> But beyond that, education ministers intimately to ultimate ends, in developing man's capacity to understand, to contemplate and to create. And it is a characteristic of the aspirations of this age to feel that, where there is capacity to pursue such activities, there that capacity should be fostered. The good society desires equality of opportunity for its citizens to become not merely good producers but also good men and women.
>
> (Robbins Report on Higher Education Vol 1 1963 p 8.)

To realize these ambitions, the Robbins Report set targets for places needed within two time phases, by 1973-74 and by 1980-81, using the strategies already outlined in Chapter 1.

	Univer-sities	Colleges of Education	Further Education	All Higher Education
England and Wales				
1962/63 (actual)	108	49	28	185
1973/74	179	111	45	335
1980/81	291	131	59	481
Scotland				
1962/63 (actual)	22	6	3	31
1973/74	40	11	6	57
1980/81	55	15	7	77
Great Britain				
1962/63 (actual)	130	55	31	216
1973/74	219	122	51	392
1980/81	346	146	66	558

(Robbins Report on Higher Education Vol 1 p 160.)

Subsequently the White Paper 'Education: a framework for Expansion' recommended in 1972 that the target for British higher education should be 750,000 students by 1981/82. (This was a slight reduction from numbers quoted in a Government Planning Paper published in 1970.)

In spite of the rapid expansion in the numbers of universities in the 1960s and early 1970s through new building programmes and upgrading of existing institutions, the Robbins Report target of 346,000 students in universities by 1980/81 had still not been achieved by 1987/88 when 320,920 students were attending United Kingdom universities. (This figure incorporates the Northern Ireland intakes at University of Ulster and the Queen's University of Belfast.)

The admissions figures for the decade of the 1980s reflect the fact that (other than the notable merger of the New University of Ulster and Ulster Polytechnic in 1984!) no new Charters had been granted.

As indicated in Table A (page 45), the number of full-time students undertaking undergraduate and postgraduate study in United Kingdom universities in 1987/88 was 320,920, representing an increase of 14,306 compared with 1980/81 figures. 41.3 % of the students in 1987/88 were women compared with 37.7% in 1980/81. The numbers of European Community students had risen by 5,026 over the 7 year period and 4,357 additional overseas students were studying on the campuses.

Of the 47,475 new entrants at undergraduate level during the 1987/88 academic year, 43.6% were women. In 1980/81, female students represented 40.4% of new entrants. 12% of all the new students in 1987/88 were 21 years of age or older which compared with 10.4% in the same age category in 1980/81.

According to OECD statistics for 1988, the rate of participation of first-time entrants to universities in the United Kingdom was 15% compared with 15.8% in Ireland. The highest participation rates in industrially advanced democracies were in Australia (50.4%), United States (47.5%) and Spain (36.6%). A further 6.2% in Britain and 15.1% in Ireland were participating in non-university tertiary education. (See Appendix II.)

Table A

All Full-time Students (Undergraduate and Postgraduate) in United Kingdom Universities 1980/81 and 1987/88

	Total		Men		Women	
	80/81	87/88	80/81	87/88	80/81	87/88
Total	306,614	320,920	190,923	188,246	115,691	132,674
Area of Domicile						
United Kingdom	270,442	275,365	164,087	157,281	106,355	118,084
Other European Community	2,529	7,555	1,416	4,329	1,113	3,226
Other Overseas	33,643	38,000	25,420	26,636	8,223	11,364

(Sources: UGC University Statistics 1987/88 Vol 1; University Statistical Record pps 14 & 15; UGC University Statistics 1980/81 University Statistical Record pps 10 & 11.)

Age at 31st August 1980 and 31st August 1987 of UK domiciled students in United Kingdom Universities as New Entrants

	TOTAL		MEN		WOMEN	
	1980	1987	1980	1987	1980	1987
18 and under	50,890	47,475	29,327	26,505	21,563	20,970
19	16,448	16,826	10,692	9,780	5,756	7,046
20	2,932	3,176	1,908	1,927	1,024	1,249
21 – 24	4,124	4,324	2,771	2,806	1,353	1,518
25 – 29	1,818	2,175	1,048	1,167	770	1,008
30 and over	2,174	2,713	993	1,107	1,181	1,606

(Sources: UGC University Statistics 1987/88 Vol 1 Universities Statistical Record pps 16 & 17 UGC University Statistics 1980 Vol 1 Universities Statistical Record pps 10 & 11.)

A succinct perspective on admissions to universities over the last twenty five years is provided by Scott:

> The social base of the universities has been broadened, but not as much as many had hoped. Going to university has become a much more common experience for 18-year-olds in Britain; indeed it has become the almost automatic expectation of many middle-class professional families. Yet the proportion of university students from working class homes has remained

> stuck at 25%. In another sense the social base of the universities has shrunk. Since 1945 most have allowed their local roots to wither. They have ceased to make a vital contribution to that civic culture of which so many universities were a product, which has diminished both the universities and that culture.   (P Scott 1984 p 210.)

In mitigation, Scott goes on to argue however that while other British institutions have been in relative decline, the universities have at least maintained an overall reputation for creativity and academic excellence and therefore must be doing something right!

With regard to the issue of the social class composition of the student population, it could be argued that the failure to make inroads has been not so much a fault of the universities themselves but is rooted in the structures of the primary and secondary schooling systems:

> At present the children of the rich have all the advantages. They have the material backing, the educated parents and the schools in the nicest areas. They are placed in schools, and streams within schools, that have an academic bent. They speak the same language as teachers and hear it in their homes. It is slanted towards examination success and higher education. The children of the poor are liable to receive little backing, a less academic curriculum and the prospect of an education finishing at 16.
>
> (M Shipman 1984 p 203.)

The theme is taken up by Osborne et al who argue that, while great gains have been achieved in opening up access since the beginning of the century, "the pernicious effects of class background remain significant." (R D Osborne, R J Cormack & R L Miller 1987 p 11.)

Yet it is in the interests of the universities, given the present constraints on budgets, to set up and run academic courses which are marketable and in line with democratic trends and the community-felt needs. This represents a genuine opportunity to promote the interests of many sections of the population who have had to endure varying degrees of social injustice.

Universal Access

It is indeed arguable that everybody should have a right at some time in their lives to the equivalent of three years of higher education. This right of access could be adopted as a standing principle and as a parallel process people could be counselled by academic staff, that, while they were entitled to enter university on a full or part-time basis, it would be the university's opinion that they would not benefit from higher education, and that they would be better off pursuing other activities. Within this model it would be left up to the individuals as to whether they wanted to pursue their academic study or not. Obviously they would have to run the risk of failing in the first year and perhaps being required to discontinue their studies. It would be important through counselling that they at least had an awareness that they might subject themselves to a form of self-damage which in the long run might be destructive. Notwithstanding this would introduce a universal right of entry into higher education. Indeed the desirability of adopting this type of flexibility in admission criteria is reinforced by the evidence which is accumulating to demonstrate that many people who hitherto have been excluded but who have been admitted on non-traditional criteria have in fact made a very valuable contribution to university life. It is morally indefensible that any student with the intellectual capacity should be prevented from pursuing higher education because of obstacles such as lack of money, or lack of opportunity arising from background, be it religion, race, creed, age or sex. Universities should be continually working at removing these barriers. They need to create opportunities for individuals to exercise that universal right of entry. It would of course be crucial not to set up another form of latent elitism, whereby those students who survived within the system were regarded as inherently better citizens whereas those who failed became viewed as stigmatized inadequates with no alternative future. Indeed the higher education system must apply the principle of transferability not just within its own system but between higher education and further education, and between modes of study – full-time, part-time; degrees, diplomas, certificates; or modules of study self-sufficient in their own right which students could undertake for general broadening of the mind rather than academic qualifications. Furthermore, to make part-time study truly feasible for many people, it is important to keep the campus open for evening classes. Warnock suggests the interesting concept of a 'sweet trolley' model, whereby any member of the public would be able to select modules and modes of study from a wide range of possibilities to make up a form of appetizing academic melange which suited their own personal needs and interests. (M Warnock 1988 p 146).

Higher education institutions have a very definite pragmatic reason, in addition to any altruistic motivation, to widen the involvement of the outside population beyond the conventional school-leaver. The demographic trends in Britain as a whole dictate that there must be a great influx of mature students and overseas or EEC students to compensate for a threatened reduction in school-leavers numbers (albeit in lower socio-economic groups) and consequent loss of revenue normally accrued through tuition fees. This opens up really progressive possibilities to alter the balance within the higher education student population to everyone's advantage. However there has to be a reciprocal responsibility on the part of the universities to work continuously at improving their insights into the needs of the growing proportion of non-traditional entrants.

The Learning Needs of Mature Students

It is a matter of debate as to whether mature students have special definable educational needs which do not also apply to school-leavers. What is a mature student? Technically it is usual to classify in this way any applicant over the age of twenty one who has been self-supporting and/or in full-time education for at least three years. Undoubtedly, over the next decade, third level institutions are going to be actively seeking to recruit such candidates to meet the demands for wider access being promulgated by the Government. The heterogeneous climate which these changing trends will introduce will be an enriching and invigorating one. Most tutors agree that mature students are a joy to teach in the sense that their level of participation is high, arising from a combination of their wider life experience and their great personal investment in entering higher education. It is arguable that they do have special needs associated with their particular backgrounds. Entry into higher education can mean a massive shift in the social roles undertaken by the individual. The former full-time worker (often at the last minute) becomes a full-time student; the income drops considerably but responsibilities remain such as family commitment, mortgages, school fees, clothing for the children, the continuing life-style of the spouse who may or may not be sympathetic to the decision to pursue a degree. It means sometimes a radical shift in identity terms. The existing peer group and social network may abruptly be severed and the process of replacing it is by no means straightforward as a mature student surrounded in a lecture theatre by eighteen and nineteen-year-olds. Sadly many third level entrants choose 'second chance' education arising out of frustration in the throes of long-term unemployment or coping with the trauma of redundancy after years of continuous work. Unlike the school-leaver, they may have long since lost the discipline or ritual of personal study and this means a series of adjustments have to be made. The very academic lecturer, on whose experience and knowledge much depends, may be years younger than the mature student and it is sometimes by no means easy to work out an appropriate way to relate to this new key figure. Is the lecturer a friend, an assessor, an authoritative teacher? In effect it probably entails a combination of all these roles but if the relationship is going to be productive and mutually rewarding one both parties have to work out the terms of the engagement. Change in income can be a corrosive factor especially if compounded by a delay in the administration of the education authority grant, because of Inland Revenue or income assessment complications. At an early stage the mature student will feel pressured to adopt an approach to study which is going to meet all deadlines and academic expectations. Essay titles or projects with hand-in dates, reading lists even if carefully trimmed by the tutor, can all present intimidating signals to the mature student. Books can quickly become dominating monsters which sap the confidence of the reader because they appear interminable and the content is not being retained even after the most assiduous periods of study. The structure of essays can pose problems; even decisions such as when to put texts to one side, to stop writing notes and commit pen to paper, can be perplexing. Having the basic confidence to analyse information, select what one considers useful and leave material aside; to commit oneself to views and support these with evidence; to be able to distinguish confidently between good evidence and bad; the most intelligent and talented mature students can find this early period of transition testing to the point that morale can become badly dented.

In a seminar or tutorial, some mythological assumptions may have to be overcome. Many mature students are at first in awe of the seeming brightness and alertness of the school-leaver. Participation may be severely inhibited by the fear that, as a mature person, one is expected to be sensible and if an opinion is ventured it might make the mature student look foolish. In practice it is usually the case that the eighteen year old is equally overawed by the presence of mature students who so obviously have a lot more life experience and general knowledge. It is important that the seminar leader has both the sensitivity and the skill to detect such inhibitions and free people up. In theory such a heterogeneous group has a better chance of becoming positive and task-centred in its problem solving but it may have to be helped through its formative stages.

With regard to the learning process itself, adult learners often have to face considerable anxiety associated with new material arising from lectures, tutorials or reading which actually challenges assumptions they may have held for many years. To surrender a shibboleth of a lifetime takes a great act of courage and openness. In the end this is the essence of learning – being able to assimilate new meanings into your existing structures of knowledge and if necessary getting rid of some mythologies and untested assumptions. However in order that the mature student can approach this task with creative and not crippling anxiety, regular reinforcement by effective role models in the form of academic staff is vital. Otherwise the phenomenon is witnessed of the evidently talented mature student dropping out of a course and rationalizing the reasons as external rather than intrinsic to the learning process itself. This is not to say of course that external pressures such as family or job commitments do not often predominate. Rather it is arguing that the process of personal development in a profound sense can be painful and anxiety-provoking and mature students may have a special if temporary need of help in this area.

Women and 'Second-Chance' Education

Various initiatives are now taking place, in the form of special bridging courses, to encourage mature women, who have interrupted their education to bring up families, to consider higher education as a route to greater self-fulfilment. There is no doubt, however, that because of the particular sexual roles into which they have been socialized, many women have to undergo a radically different form of adjustment from men when entering third level education. Conditioned to positions of relative economic powerlessness, the self-image of the mature mother/wife may be passive and fatalistic. As a consequence, the level of self-esteem may be very low, to the extent that the woman totally underestimates her own strengths and qualities. Accustomed to 'remembering her place' in life, it can be a frightening prospect to be invited to exercise her brain as a more independent spirit. Indeed there may even be associated guilt feelings that somehow the woman is an impostor with no real right to be on the campus at all.

It is highly questionable as to whether universities are as sensitive to these issues as they might be. The model of social reality of the mature female student may have to alter fundamentally if she is to do justice to her latent academic potential. Yet the very structure within third level institutions themselves may present obstacles to this development instead of facilitating it. The continuing male dominance, particularly at senior academic and administrative levels, tells its own story about implicit bias. Demonstrably it just cannot be the case that there are not enough capable women available with the ability to manage and administer as well as to teach in the higher education context. This being so, the unpalatable likelihood is that educational institutions themselves are colluding with the perpetuating the structural inequalities that are so apparent still in wider society. As the proportion of mature women students inevitably increases on campuses, there must be a reciprocal increase in the proportion of women enabled to take up positions within the colleges at the levels where policies are formulated and implemented.

Overseas Students

In recent years there has been a mounting ethical dilemma concerning the recruitment of overseas students into British and Irish universities . As the financing of higher education has come under mounting pressure and sources of external revenue have been increasingly sought, administrators have actively courted the overseas student market and would justify this policy approach in terms of the economic survival of the institution. Ideally there are multiple benefits to be derived from the presence of overseas students. In addition to a qualification, the student gains valuable experience in studying with local and other foreign students. Allied to this is the cross-cultural experience of residing in the United Kingdom or

Ireland. From the standpoint of the institution, additional revenue is only one of many valuable consequences. The whole intellectual climate is broadened and British and Irish students have the opportunity to extend their experience and cultivate international attitudes. Potential insularity on the part of the institutions is avoided because of the cross-cultural stimulation at all levels, among staff and students. And the regional community benefits not just economically but through the enrichment of social contact and exchange. Research is invigorated and the international reputation of the educational institution is invariably elevated. At national level, there are potential improvements in trade links, exports, friendship networks and a widening of spheres of influence.

The multiple factors involved in the mutual contact between third level institutions and overseas students were succinctly summed up in a policy statement by the United Kingdom Council for Overseas Student Affairs:

> If overseas students are not to become a source of problems per se, then it is necessary to face the reality with which we are dealing; overseas students undoubtedly have greater institutional needs than home students. They make greater demands on academic and admissions staff, on health, welfare, counselling and accommodation services. Any weakness in admissions procedures, academic provision or support services will be thrown into high relief by the presence of overseas students. A corollary to this is that the effective management of policy and provision for overseas students will inform and enhance institutional practice in relation to all students. The issue is not the need to devote substantial additional resources to overseas students. The effective institution will embody a concept of total educational provision, including academic and welfare, tutoring and counselling services to the benefit of all students, which subsumes a recognition of the special needs of overseas students.

(UKCOSA 1986 p 20.)

Students with Disabilities

Widening of access should also lead to a much greater proportion of students who have special needs arising from disability. It is evident that the school system needs to examine more critically whether there is a sufficiently comprehensive attempt to educate disabled students and prepare them for continuation at third level. Are the visions in the minds of the teachers even able to encompass the possibility that profoundly deaf or blind or wheelchair-user students should have expectations at all about studying at university level? Clearly there is a limit to what colleges themselves can contribute when resources are constrained and many students are competing for these resources. Fairness and keeping a balanced perspective are important so that no-one within the general student population is disadvantaged. This has clear implications for the ways in which budgets are prioritized. At best institutions can try to smooth individualized paths for disabled students into higher education and rally round to provide facilities and support services on an 'ad hoc' basis. Perhaps there is a case for some establishments developing specialized facilities to which disabled applicants could be referred. This already happens to some extent (eg at Southampton University). The risk that may have to be faced here though is that of stigmatization of disabled students through segregation. Integration into full campus life might be preferred as the ideal approach. But the unpalatable fact remains that many disabled students never proceed beyond CSE or GCSE Level, not because of lack of intellectual potential, but because the physical and practical obstacles to progress tend to engender a fatalistic attitude in the teacher as well as in the student. Furthermore, if students with disability enter higher education, they may still have to contend with attitudes that are less than helpful:

> Not only is it necessary to improve the level of facilities available, additionally, 'Staff Disability Awareness' training programmes are necessary. Lecturers have admitted to feelings of uncertainty and discomfort in teaching students with physical disabilities. (S Jones 1988 p 39.)

Postgraduate Research Students

When discussing access it is worthwhile to consider postgraduate research students as a separate and distinct category for the following reasons: they often do not have the benefit of peer group support which undergraduates or graduates on taught courses tend to have; they may be returning to studies after a gap during which they were doing other unrelated things; they may be entering the particular institution for a first time and thus be going through a process of adjustment to a strange environment not dissimilar to the school-leaver. It is acknowledged of course that they would on the other hand tend to have much more sophistication in their understanding of the ways of the higher education world. However postgraduate research sets up its own peculiar demands on the student. Alongside part- time seminar teaching or demonstrating, the student may be expected to contribute to a team research project where the outcome of the research is vital to the overall objectives; alternatively it may be a totally individual piece of research wherein the responsibility for its development and resolution lies with the student under appropriate supervision. The latter category can be in practice a solitary exercise in that the motivation of the student is usually high with a great investment in succeeding, but there is no natural forum in which to test out ideas other than the one to one relationship with the supervisor. Thus the quality of this relationship is vitally important and the nature and clarity of the contract agreed is absolutely crucial. There is a relatively high non-completion rate among postgraduate students and one of the core factors appears to be a decline in motivation or ability to sustain energy levels because of a loss of a sense of direction. As a route to on-going personal development, research for a higher degree is at the apex of academic life. It addresses fundamental issues about taking responsibility for your own learning, sorting out objectives, using the mental faculties of analysis, assimilation, synthesis – all the components of intellectual problem solving. By the very definition of a doctorate as a symbol of excellence and creative advance made in a field of study, a certain acceptable drop-out rate or failure rate is inevitable. However by making every effort to formulate a clear initial contract with students and select supervisors who are confident in the field and sensitive to the potential isolation of the student's roles, the educational institution can ensure that mutual expectations are realistic from the outset. Students can then be self-selecting in deciding whether this is a route that is appropriate for the next stage of their personal development.

Funding of Higher Education

Everyone has a right to a taste of higher education; consequently universities should be portrayed as a public service not dependent upon privilege. It follows therefore that the financing of third level education should come predominantly from public funds. At the same time academic institutions make a substantial contribution to private economic development. The profitability of business and commerce in a sense is underwritten by the provision of knowledge intensive labour in the form of university graduates – a form of 'human capital'. There is a case therefore for introducing a special higher education levy onto the larger corporations in order to increase the funding available to colleges.

Notwithstanding it is imperative that academic institutions should have sufficient public funding to fulfil the objectives of their Charter or Mission Statement. This would guarantee a security to universities and underwrite a national commitment to their role in wider society. Similar to the National Health Service (in its original form), the funding would be achieved through national taxation and government budget allocation.

There is no doubt that a move towards an imbalance in the form of private funding would further disadvantage people who have been traditionally disadvantaged in relation to pursuing academic careers.

Perhaps government, higher education and industry should establish a more comprehensive liaison or co-ordination as 'branches' of society. Businesses could be encouraged to support good universities as positive 'causes' which help produce their future 'human capital'. The enterprise culture is a modern reality but it would not be healthy if colleges unquestioningly had to provide anything that entrepreneurs paid for, as the element of general educative purpose within higher education would be lost. Humanities and philosophy for instance would struggle to find financial benefactors in today's economic climate. The private purse tends to focus on technological interests, and ventures which are open to commercial exploitation.

Perhaps three quarters of funding should come from public funds and one quarter from private funds as a form of healthy balance. It might even be feasible to have public funding in two forms: (a) the baseline grant to keep establishments functioning; and (b) competitive money where universities bid to sell their skills to government departments. If they wanted a contract to be undertaken, the government departments would place it with the successful college. For instance, the Department of the Environment might accord a contract to the University Environmental Science Department. The money thus gained could subsidize teaching and research, field trips for students. Students themselves could work on the contracts, six weeks here, two months there, getting to know departmental functions, roles of staff, networks of communication, the disciplines of working to committee deadlines. This would be neither private funding nor government direct funding but would have healthy ingredients from both.

Baseline funding would be important to maintain the fabric of the academic institution. Some areas are particularly open to private 'top-up' funding – for instance product development, medicine. On the other hand the government contract funding referred to above would not be in the form of set grants – colleges would have to create the required products in order to keep the money coming in and would indeed have to be good at the job they were doing to have future contracts renewed. This could be a more integrated way of doing things – and would certainly be an answer to some of the criticisms that money is poured down a cosmic black hole when given to higher education. Nonetheless there must be a government commitment for funding the universities either through contracts or baseline support in order to support their fundamental integrity.

Students' Financial Support

It has been postulated in this book that universities must continue to grow as a public service and if the projected figures are realistic, they will provide education for over one third of all school-leavers by the end of the century. It is also manifestly clear, as already discussed, that an increasing proportion of the future student intake will of necessity have to be mature students if target figures are to be realized alongside the effects of the drop in birth rate. Yet the current government appears to be building in a contradictory blocking mechanism by its decision to freeze student grants and introduce a top-up student loan scheme. Fatuous comparisons are being made with higher education in the United States to justify the feasibility of such a scheme. It would appear that, ultimately, the future of the entire mandatory grant system is in jeopardy and increasingly students will have to regard their higher education as a self-financing exercise, the costs of which may be repaid over an elastically extended number of years.

As a parallel process alongside the principles being espoused within this book for a comprehensive approach to the personal development of people, this political decision will be disastrously counter-productive. Britain has relatively low wage rates compared with other European countries and the United States and there is no automatic guarantee nowadays of a certain career route into many of the professions for graduates. Even if a procedure is worked out with the banking institutions for a specially deflated rate of interest, the student applicant will have to undertake, at the point of entry, an immediate debt which will have an array of social and emotional implications. Given the wide range of backgrounds of potential future students and the existing personal commitments that they will inevitably carry, this must create considerable additional pressure. Going through the transition into full- time studentship immediately has substantial costs, be it for second home accommodation, travel, subsistence, course materials. Should the acquired loan be insufficient, the student is also faced with the prospect of having to approach the administration of the university for an Access Fund grant or loan out of the government's contingency fund. However while these Funds have been made available on a differentiated basis in accordance with student population sizes, they do not begin to compensate for other structural changes. Principally, the right to DHSS benefit has now been withdrawn from single undergraduates, as has entitlement to housing benefit.

Warnock urges that the government should revert to the spirit of the Robbins Report:

> It is unthinkable that any government should altogether go back on such a commitment. Student grants are mandatory: students are not luxuriously provided for: indeed government itself has admitted that their grants, severely cut in real terms since the beginning of the 1980s, are no longer adequate. — so there is no way out of it: higher education must be paid for publicly.   (M Warnock 1988 p 136.)

This seems an eminently sensible argument. However, if the goal of facilitating the personal development of an increasingly wide cross-section of citizens is going to be tackled in a profound way over the next twenty five years, even more extensive commitment of the public purse to the mandatory grant system is required. Parental assessment should be totally abolished and every student over the age of eighteen years should be entitled to a full index-linked living allowance within their grants. It is a total contradiction in terms on the one hand to be urging students to engage in critical adult dialogue and on the other hand keeping many of the students in a repressed state of childlike dependency on parental contributions, which may or may not be forthcoming.

There has to be an act of faith that, as universities proceed to educate greater numbers of the citizenry, there will be an infinite range of benefits to the wider society which will more than recompense the taxpayers for their outlay. This honouring of the social contract by higher education will be reflected not just in the workaday skills and competencies of the graduates, but in the richness and optimistic vision of the ideas which will permeate the whole social system.

Failure to review and move away from this current political expedition into student loans will not only in time reveal the falseness of the economies, but will have catastrophic social consequences. It will be deeply divisive in that many talented people from lower income backgrounds will decide against applying for a third level place in the first instance. Many existing students will be condemned to a plight where anxieties about the stigma of debt and the dangers of defaulting may well detract from the primary goal of realizing their full potential academically. Furthermore the universities will once again be perceived in the public eye as aloof finishing schools for the wealthy, to which the talented poor may be admitted as a privilege.

Because of its limited student grant system, the Republic of Ireland faces similar decisions about the future structuring of income support for higher education students. A critical evaluation of the British and American loan schemes is essential. There is growing evidence to suggest that the administrative costs in operating the schemes and following up defaulters are bound to escalate. A proper investment in higher education is required, not short-term false economies.

Chapter Four

Facilitating the Intellectual and Personal Development of Students

Freedom to Learn

Objectivity is a desirable quality and students must try to develop a respect for facts, standards of honesty in the treatment of evidence. But it is quite absurd to maintain that the educational process can be based on some form of total neutrality and impartiality. Indeed, in the past, such illusory assertions have been used as a dismissal or isolation of theories and ideas labelled as unconventional or unorthodox. It is a reasonable expectation that third level institutions should attempt to take up neutral stances between ideological positions, but it is quite misplaced to expect that this could apply to individuals. In practice, it is vital to provide the academic freedom for and tolerance of a wide variety of commitments, approaches, even biases among academic educators. Arising from this, students can then positively develop potential for self-direction and independence of thought. Education should be required to be:

> ... a constant process of self-criticism, directed above all at the ideological orthodoxies which invariably play a large part in determining both what is taught and how it is taught. For education, of course, stands outside society in this respect. (A Arblaster 1974.)

This concern to retain academic freedom is in the interests both of the students and the wider society. Freedom to formulate and expound ideas and opinions, which are not part of current orthodoxy is acutely important for the preservation of democratic values of change and reforms by popular consent. In contrast, intolerance or suppression of such ideas is usually a clear indicator of a state which has achieved or has aspirations towards authoritarian dominance. Consequently the struggle by educators to retain the protected right for dissident and untrammelled thinking is in fact a cause held in common with all citizens concerned about libertarian issues.

Education as Transformation

There is a process of change or transformation which should be evident in the student who progresses through higher education. In the realm of ideas the student has the opportunity to become liberated from the mental clutter which has accumulated from birth. This clutter consists of the passed on assumptions which are culture bound or even peculiar to the immediate locality; the mythologies which make up the legend, custom and practice of the particular grouping; the fears and taboos which people often allow to dominate their actions but are unable to articulate and bring to overt consciousness; the normative expectations which are the ingredients of social control. While many of these features are functional in that they ensure an equilibrium for the society or community in question, they are by their very nature restrictive. They may affirm homeostasis but they do not encourage growth. For instance the group may find common support in identifying a mutual enemy and attributing all sorts of historical negative attributes to that enemy; but if there is no means to overcome this prejudicial state, or indeed desire to do so, the understanding by that group of the world around can only be restricted and distorted.

One way of describing the transformation that higher education can facilitate is the increased capacity of the individual to move from an inward looking self-obsessed model of reality to one where the existence of other sets of ideas is profoundly recognized. The 'I' as the centre of the universe is replaced by a curiosity that there is a rich admixture of beings in the world with different frames of reference and ideas to which labels of 'right' and 'wrong', 'valid' and 'invalid' are just not applicable. Egocentrism becomes replaced by a more humble and liberating recognition that there is a wide array of ways in which to view the world and define the issues within it. In the academic setting, the student becomes aware of the possibility of reaching intellectual consensus on certain issues, or on the other hand accepting conflicts that remain unresolved – it could be that this is the first awakening to the fact that external views exist outside the student's own subjectivity which demand that they must be listened to with tolerance and critical judgement.

> The University is a Mecca to which students come with something less than perfect faith. It is important that students bring a certain ragamuffin, barefoot irreverence to their studies; they are not here to worship what is known but to question it.   (J Bronowski 1973 p 360.)

Another feature of educational transformation is its emancipating force. The entrant to higher education may have been hitherto a 'minor', having been dependent and not entitled to make autonomous decisions. It may be the school-leaver who is literally establishing an identity away from the nuclear family for the first time. Old inherited values have been held in question or rejected but the individual is still going through the process of sorting out the ultimate principles of living that make personal sense. Education can provide the touchstone in an unbiased manner by providing novel perspectives and actually encouraging critical reflection. This re-examination or reshaping of the individual's identity may also be an important feature of the mature adult learner who is returning to full-time education after a gap of some years. Perhaps the earlier school experience was even damaging, confidence and esteem being diminished by the style of teaching or the uncaring attitude encountered. It could be that the individual has undertaken a working career in industry only to discover that redundancy has stripped away old roles, causing a new normlessness and crisis of identity. The examination of old assumptions, potentially a painful and uncomfortable experience as it is venturing into the unknown, can also have the substantial reward of a greater clarity of perspective, an unmuddying of the waters.

Thus higher education can literally transform self-image, equip the individual with more skills, build on the basis of the knowledge that the individual had before arrival; change attitudes and assumptions. Indeed higher education can restore the will in the student to continue personal development after previous negative messages. The educational process can mean empowerment. It instils qualities of flexibility, adaptability and confidence and the capacity to keep changing within a changing society. The critical questioning attitudes which the academic institution encourages equips the student to carry on the emancipation process afterwards into the wider society. As a result of higher education the student should be freer intellectually and able to question the constraints on pursuit of knowledge, hindrances to human enjoyment and obstacles to freedom.

Without becoming too grandiose, a university can help transform the raw material in the individual into a 'civilized' mind – a mind with taste, discrimination and sound judgement, capable of certain skills and competencies in the evaluation of evidence, assessment of arguments. The individual not only has more knowledge but has the discipline of being able to apply that knowledge and the preparedness to accept responsibility for the application of that knowledge. The individual has also developed a rigour in terms of values, attitudes and behaviour. Hopefully tolerance and humility figure prominently within such values. In addition the personal development involved goes far beyond the intellectual plane. It also involves the expressive, emotional and physical development of the person. Development of inter-personal skills and learning, how to work with other people in a group context, can also transform the individual student from an introspective stance. This is crucial in order to develop real decision-making ability through the harnessing of group resources.

In contrast to authoritarian transmission of pre-packaged 'knowledge' to passive learners, this process of education requires a democratized model of learning. Such a democratic approach refutes the assumption that whatever is taught is automatically what is learnt. It is not possible to implant an educational process within an individual. The art of the academic educators must be to facilitate the learning of the students. With regard to the goals of democratic education, the emphasis on growth expounded by Rogers is appropriate.

- to assist students to become individuals who are able to take self-initiated action and to be responsible for those actions;
- who are capable of intelligent choice and self-direction;
- who are critical learners, able to evaluate the contributions made by others;
- who have acquired knowledge relevant to the solution of problems;
- who, even more importantly, are able to adapt flexibly and intelligently to new problem situations;
- who have internalized an adaptive mode of approach to problems, utilizing all pertinent experience freely and creatively;
- who work, not for the approval of others, but in terms of their own socialized purposes.

(C R Rogers 1973 pps 387/388.)

In essence, higher education should involve critical reflection, positive action, and untrammelled use of the creative imagination. At the same time, the process of higher education represents a form of mediation between two very fluid and potentially conflicting values – the personal values of the individual pursuing self-development and the communal values of the society in which the individual has to live and contribute:

Life is the woof of self-expression crossing the warp of social values and education in the attempt to make life more complete and satisfying.

(McCallister 1931 p 12.)

Measurement of 'Value-Added'

Following the publication of the Jarratt Report (1985), British higher education was left in no doubt about the expectations emanating from government for greater efficiency in management. To give practices a more coherent structure, it was recommended that academic managers should monitor and measure performance in the various sectors of activity with reference to 'performance indicators'. In the plethora of consultative documents and academic publications which followed, several indicators were identified. They include measurement of: degree results; cost per student or staff-student ratio; wastage and non-completion rates; employment after graduation; research quality and income; publications and patents; student evaluation; peer reviews; reputational ranking; quality of input by entry qualification. Essentially these are becoming the tools of the managers in their efforts to provide evidence of effective and efficient practice.

However it is notable that there has been a lack of detailed precision in any discussion of the performance indicator which has come to be labelled as 'value-added'. What is the nature of the 'value-added' by the higher education process? Two school-leavers, for instance, who are closely similar in attainment and ability decide to pursue different career routes, one entering higher education and the other going into industry. How can an accurate measurement be made of the capacity of the academic establishment to influence positively the intellectual and personal development of the student? And what is the 'value-added' by the degree in terms of the ultimate contribution of that student to the welfare and advancement of society compared with his peer who entered the world of work directly.

> Education is of value to the individual in terms of the consumption benefits
> of undergoing it, the pecuniary advantage of increasing earnings potential
> and other benefits in terms of personal development.
>
> (Cave, Hanney, Kogan & Trevett 1988 p 59.)

In terms of effective management, one institution can claim to be relatively more efficient than others if it can accomplish more value-added benefits for the student at the same or lower cost. When a ratio is worked out of average value-added benefit to average cost, then the higher the ratio, the more efficient the college. At a time when there appears to be almost an obsessional preoccupation with quantification and downward transmission management in the higher education sector, this may appear to be a potentially soulless and mechanistic line to pursue. However the discipline of establishing a clear set of qualitative measures which highlight the nature of the transformation of the student through the process of higher education could also be a means of validating and celebrating the third level experience. Perhaps criticisms in the past that some higher education institutions have been too insular, mystical and esoteric have had some justification. It is in the interests of future students that more coherent ways of assessing the developmental experience are constructed. Only by lucidly outlining the components that constitute the 'value-added' by the educational experience, can the academic teams and support services plan to replicate or improve that experience for future cohorts of students.

Value-added components are in fact easily identified in global terms. These can be summarized as:

    (a)   gains in knowledge and improvement in skills;

    (b)   extent of personal development.

Difficulties are inevitably encountered however when making choices of means of measurement which are neither too ambiguous nor lead to serious distortions. For the remainder of this chapter, an attempt will be made to examine more closely these central components of 'value-added' and to identify some of the variables which influence the quality of the student experience.

(a) Gains in Knowledge and Improvement in Skills

Obviously the ultimate degree classification achieved by the student is a major indicator of the expansion of the individual's knowledge base. With caution, attempts can be made to measure the difference between the degree result and the original entry qualifications of the student. However as baseline measures, entry qualifications are notoriously problematical. If a student enters a third level institution with very high scores, this could produce an artificially low value-added rating on completion of the course. And it is noteworthy that there will be an increasing proportion of mature students entering higher education in the years ahead who will not have conventional qualifications for entry. This will place an additional importance on selection interviews and the ability of the admission tutors or their administrative equivalent to assess the existent knowledge base of the mature applicant.

This issue of identifying the starting baseline of co-operation of the student and measuring the extent of transformation raises unavoidable questions about the extent of insight and supportiveness within the course teaching teams. To what extent are seminars organized to facilitate face-to-face small group discussion alongside the traditional lecture transmission? Do seminar leaders think through sufficiently the objectives of their sessions and consciously bring into play techniques to encourage balanced participation and take account of individual stages of learning? Are students introduced to studies advisers at an early stage of their studies and enabled to develop a rapport on an individual adult-to-adult basis? The most satisfactory working definition of an effective studies adviser is one who can help remove obstacles in the way of academic progress and the realization of individual academic potential. It should be the duty of the adviser to gauge the knowledge baseline of the student at an early stage and literally to record the strengths and weaknesses exhibited by the student throughout the academic year. Indeed a little sensitive intervention at a crucial stage, for instance in giving advice about adopting a personally suitable study style, can be of immense long-term value. Some bureaucracy is inevitable in the sense that, ideally, studies advisers should be completing progress forms, jointly with the full knowledge of the student, on a termly basis and then at the end of the academic year presenting an academic profile to the Examination Board which is considering progress or eventual award. Reports from studies advisers should include some analysis of results of continuous or intermittent assessment work such as essays or laboratory work. Were the results compatible with the early academic indicators of potential? What form of adjustments had to be made in the course of the year, for instance if the student is from overseas or a 'second chance' mature student? Were there any relevant mitigating circumstances if work was not completed on time or fell below expected grades? What decisions had the student arrived at in relation to choice of subject for further study and on the basis of what criteria?

In the past there has been a quite unforgivable tendency among some academic tutors to dismiss this form of supportive contact with students as unnecessary pandering. The arrogance which usually underlies such assertions is that students have to learn quickly as part of their development and this is expedited if the crude message from the Faculty is 'Sink or Swim!' Such insensitive and smug attitudes have undoubtedly greatly hampered the learning process of many able students in the past who had the potential and aptitude for academic fulfilment but just required the encouragement and fostering of self-confidence.

With insightful co-ordination within Faculties, an effective studies advice system can be organised and maintained without inflationary resource implications.

The Primary Skills of the University Teacher

There are several key areas where a high order of ability on the part of the tutor is crucial if the learning process is to be facilitated adequately. Although these are presented in linear fashion for the sake of clarity, it is also vital that the tutor has the insight to select a method or battery of methods that are appropriate to the particular goals and the stages of learning of the students.

Lecturing

Given that this most economical method of communication is likely to remain as a traditional method in the expanding higher education system, it is essential that the lecture is only utilized with the clearest possible objectives in mind. Optimal benefit is derived when the lecture is used to: provide a structure for a field of knowledge; discuss the main issues in an enquiry; outline key ideas that have emerged in a particular discipline area and identify the evidence used to support the arguments which give direction to that field of knowledge; present a synoptic view which develops a students' understanding and saves time; illustrate a thesis and antithesis and invite the student to take up opinions within the debate.

In order to achieve the goals of coverage of material, generation of understanding, and maintaining the interest and motivation of the student, the lecturer must make the presentation clear and of lively interest and must demonstrate a central skill of explanation. Underpinning this process is careful advance preparation and thoughtful supplementary use of audio-visual aids and hand-outs. Enthusiastic expressiveness is also vital. In order to improve continually, the good lecturer takes regular feedback and evaluation from the students, both orally and in written form. Of course the absolute prerequisite is that the lecturer has a constantly updated and secure knowledge base and confident interest in his or her field of study!

In his classic text, Bligh summarizes the limitations in the use of lectures:

> It is concluded that they can be used to teach information, including the framework of a subject, but an expository approach is unsuitable to stimulate thought or to change attitudes. While it is not normally possible to establish rules of lecturing technique, some suggestions are made in the light of psychological and experimental evidence, on ways of organizing information, teaching a single idea, using hand-outs and feedback techniques and overcoming common difficulties. In each case preparation is required to follow these suggestions.

> It has been argued that the limitations of the lecture method commonly necessitate its use in combination with other methods. The way methods are combined also requires preparation in the light of the objectives to be achieved. (D A Bligh 1972 p 192.)

Small Group Teaching

Small groups (up to a maximum of twenty) are usually the best forum in which to set up a creative exchange as they enable the greatest amount of personal interaction. Particularly at an early stage of the student's academic career they also provide opportunities to instil confidence to help with adjustment, and adaptation to a new academic setting which in many ways may be foreign to the student. One of the first tasks of the tutor may be to give the students the confidence even to open their mouths and express opinions when their previous educational experience has tended not to reinforce this type of initiative. If real intellectual development is to take place at all, the tutor, in a sense, must be able to, 'wean' the student away from the notion that one has to sit in front of the teacher, laboriously take down everything that is said and wait for instructions to leave. The object of good teaching is to instil the enthusiasm to go out and explore.

The group analyses and evaluates each member's contribution to the solution of the problem, and various contributions are synthesized into a final group product. Individual members gather information and ideas to present to the group, but all members co-operate in analyzing the information and weaving it into a meaningful statement. — The analysis, synthesis and evaluation of information and ideas are generally acknowledged to constitute higher levels of intellectual functioning than those required of students when asked to acquire and understand given quantities of knowledge.

(Sharan and Sharan 1976 p 12.)

In order to promote thinking and discussion skills in students, tutors themselves need to give structured leadership to the small group to maximize its potential. Of a high premium in this context are questioning and listening skills. Allied to these, the lecturer must be able to respond appropriately, to summarize the range of discussion, and to effect a closure of a session. It is highly significant in terms of a student group's morale and sense of worth whether a group session has been ended with an appraisal of results achieved and acknowledgement of the positive contribution of the members.

Experimentation in the use of small groups is also potentially productive at a time when academic staff resources are not expanding. For instance, it can foster a sense of mutual support if tutors encourage small groups to work on tasks independently on alternate weeks, or 'syndicate' groups are established to take on particular projects independently and report later to plenary sessions.

Laboratory Teaching

The fundamental objective of the tutor should be to help students teach themselves and assist each other in a mutual learning process. Obviously, an essential backcloth to enable this to happen is the efficient advance preparation of experiments, outline of tasks and provision of guidelines or manuals by the lecturers or demonstrators. Explicit aims, clear instructions, well-produced illustrations, slides or graphs, identification of key questions, and self-evaluation check lists are essential keys to effective learning and must be provided rigorously by the lecturer.

Research Supervision

The tutor must have clear ideas about the structuring and planning of supervision of research students. The ability to give appropriate feedback is central in order to set unambiguous criteria of performance, to assist the student in improving research methods, to reinforce constructive achievement and to help deepen understanding of the materials. Because of the interpersonal nature of the supervision, the tutor must make early and genuine efforts to establish a good rapport.

Empathic Skills

In all areas of teaching and supervision, the lecturer must be able to demonstrate a real interest in the welfare and personal development of the students. A detached mechanistic approach to education is inappropriate for adult learners in higher education. The foundations for a good relaxed climate for learning can be set at an early stage through expression of basic concerns about settling in and transition and the outlining of the future programme of work in a straightforward and unthreatening way.

Ultimately the student has to be convinced that learning and change are inherently of value in themselves. This is the opposite side of the coin from a form of collusion which can take place whereby, at a sentient level, the tutor and the student are basically concluding that 'education' is a transmission process leading to examinations in which regurgitation will gain a pass. This can actually prevent the student from developing a thirst for knowledge, from being excited about new learning. In practice the technique primarily taught is mechanistic; guessing questions to be set in examinations, but not actually concerned about the content and quality of the learning. In contrast some students do arrive on campus having acquired that respect for learning through family, friends, personality or personal interest. Other students can only acquire that insight, motivation or love of knowledge or ability to seek further information with the help of interested tutors who convey their own inherent belief in the process.

Among ways of conveying such attitudes is a democratized approach with the group of students. Unfortunately negative images abound of tutors who do not like to be challenged and who, even more reprehensively, tell students in contradictory fashion to interrupt and then become irate when students take them at their word.

Tutorial Skills

Tutorial skills with individual students represent an important form of communication. In this context the studies adviser can explore how the students are feeling about academic life, how they are integrating new knowledge into their ongoing studies, how the acquisition of knowledge is impacting on them.

At all times the studies adviser needs to have the needs of students in mind. And the needs are not just in the terms of intellectual capacity to grasp the subject. There are many problems within the biographical map that students carry around them that affect academic ability and performance and may be exerting pressure upon them. Studies advisers should be receptive to cues about such matters and be prepared to help the student remove any obstacles in the way of their academic progress. At the same time it is acknowledged that while the relationship between the studies adviser and student is not entirely a relationship of equality, and it is recognized that, existentially, students do not know as much as the tutors in most instances, the aim should be to have mutual interchange openly and without feelings of threat. Excessive consciousness of status and hierarchy would quickly and easily upset this process.

It is important to recognize that the requirements of study and reading are ultimately a lonely occupation. Real progress is made in grappling with subject matter, mastering and understanding it, seeing flaws in it and being able to criticize it, when the student engages in study and reflection at an intellectual level independently and alone. Ideas can of course be exchanged with friends, or debated in group tutorials. But the intellectual achievement involved cannot be accomplished solely as a group exercise. Intellectual growth does have an essential element of uniqueness and solitariness. Indeed whether one refers to a school-leaver or to a mature student it will probably be extremely beneficial if the implications of this very fact were discussed in detail at an early stage of their academic career with their studies advisers.

Study Skills

It is a fundamental prerequisite that tutors must have or gain perspicacious awareness of the principles and time phases of study. Furthermore one of the greatest gifts which can be bestowed on a student is the transferring of that awareness through role modelling so that the student can in effect take on full personal responsibility for his or her own learning. This precious acquisition is one which will not only be applied with enthusiasm and success to the specific matter of academic study but will be generalized in its usefulness when the student passes through the portals of the academic institution to the wider world outside:

> Learning is essentially an active process of relating new material to old, and of establishing networks and connections within and between units of knowledge. It follows that effective learning is more likely to occur when:
>
> 1. The lecturer accurately diagnoses what the students already knows and how that knowledge is organized.
>
> 2. The lecturer consciously designs learning tasks that build from the students' existing cognitive structures towards the new knowledge or understanding that is to be acquired.
>
> 3. New knowledge and understanding is made meaningful to the student(s) by links to personal experience or prior knowledge.
>
> 4. Students are asked in advance to select and retrieve the existing knowledge they will need to make sense of new inputs.

5. There is a match between students' preferred orientation to learning and the learning task. Or any one of a number of learning methods can be used to perform the task (eg data collection and collation, memorization, critical analysis, evaluation, restructuring, synthesizing, intuitive use of evidence, searching for underlying structure, using analogies or metaphors).

6. Students are aware of their own learning strategies and alternatives.

7. Students develop a repertoire of learning skills and strategies from direct teaching, explicit modelling by the lecturers, practice and feedback.

(G Brown & M Atkins 1988 p 160.)

Baldwin and Williams stress that, to prompt students to take responsibility for their own active learning, it is necessary to establish a new climate for the student group which in effect creates a learning environment. This climate has to be one which:

− provides reassurance that the learners share common ground and can make mistakes without fear of humiliation;

− puts students in touch with the fact that they have boundless energy to invest in active learning (bearing in mind that previous educational experience may have conditioned them in the role of passive recipients of 'knowledge');

− helps students to develop mutual support in order to take risks, see challenge as useful and constructive, and realize that it is all right to acknowledge and learn from mistakes and failure;

− encourages motivation in the individual students and commitment to the group as a whole as a forum for learning in which they can take risks;

− reassures students that they can cope with the discomfort of being challenged and move into areas of uncertainty; taking themselves beyond important learning junctions;

− identifies the starting point for each individual learner, enables them to establish goals and needs and actively review their own progress; reinforces the importance of self-evaluation in the learning process;

− shifts the focus away eventually from the tutor so that the learners themselves become the centre of attention and develop a spirit of mutual help.

(J Baldwin & H Williams 1988 p 74.)

Evidently, the standards of teaching in higher education are immensely variable. Some lecturers have extensive knowledge of a subject but do not have the ability to communicate it. Others have an engaging enthusiasm but lack orderliness in their preparation and delivery. When it is considered that, unlike the school system, no formal qualifications in teaching are required at university level, this is perhaps hardly surprising. There is also evidence of differing attitudes towards students themselves. Many lecturers fortunately recognize the crucial importance of feedback and participation in terms of students' intellectual development and build these features into their teaching style. In contrast there is still a degree of remoteness in some academic staff which reflects an attitude that students are merely empty vessels to be filled with transmitted knowledge. If the students fail to learn or develop, then it is their own pathological inadequacy, and certainly not the fault of the lecturer!

If key lecturing staff are deficient in pedagogical skills, then the student becomes a trapped victim whose learning perforce has to be based on personal initiative. In such an instance, attempts to measure value-added in terms of growth in knowledge and improvement in skills become absurd. In order to gain more control over the variable of the ability of the lecturer, a number of constructive initiatives should be actively pursued.

In Russia, as part of the system of People's Universities, there are currently about 1,500 institutions designated as 'Universities of the Lecturer's Trade'. The 180,000 participants in their programmes are trained both in lecturing techniques and in the teaching of the specific material of their specializations. The philosophical framework for the courses is based on the belief that the lecturer's trade is a synthesis of four characteristics:

1. Political knowledge.
2. General cultural and specialized knowledge.
3. Pedagogical, psychological and logical knowledge and habits.
4. Mastery of the skills of oral presentations and the fundamental techniques of the orator's art.

(D C Lee 1988 p 113.)

It is greatly to be desired that such an officially organized course of study with a recognized qualification should be universally required by British and Irish institutions of higher education as a condition of appointment. Subsequent to appointment, lecturers should be obliged to participate in regular updating short courses. Faculties themselves as a matter of professional discipline should convene, at least on a termly basis, peer development seminars in which constructive critical examination can take place of the standards of teaching. This might even involve peers sitting in on each other's teaching sessions in order to be able to give direct feedback.

Staff-student consultative committees should meet at least at the end of every term to evaluate the course programmes and explicitly assess whether the predetermined contract for the course has been fulfilled. These should be formally minuted occasions with a clear mandate given to student representatives to speak frankly on behalf of fellow students. Responses should be presented in subsequent meetings to the student representatives if issues cannot be resolved instantaneously. The opportunity for students to assist in evaluating the quality of the teaching input should be recognized as an important ingredient in their personal development as adults. Should improvements be effected, the students can also directly contribute to the welfare of future students who will benefit from the changes.

On an individual level, lecturers should be encouraged to conduct regular self-appraisal in terms of the balance of their workload, their career aspirations, their contributions to the institution at large, and the effectiveness of their teaching. While a jaundiced view abounds that formal appraisal schemes which are being introduced in the higher education sector are really instruments of management control which will only generate conservative and defensive responses from staff, there is a cogent argument for harnessing regular appraisal procedures to positive staff development initiatives. If teaching is suffering for instance because of sweatshop staff-student ratios, or preoccupations with revenue-raising through selective research, then organizational priorities perhaps need to be reviewed. Evaluation of teaching performance is such a vital key to a profound educational experience for a student that it must not be shirked. Academic defensiveness or fatuous shibboleths about libertarian individualism which is above accountability, must be set aside. There is a greater responsibility to engage in a contracted educational experience in which standards of excellence give the student every opportunity for intellectual and personal development.

Integration of Theory and Practice.

Since the 1960s there has been visible strain between the advocates of purist college-based study and those who wished to pursue a more vocational and outward-looking approach. The introduction of some degree programmes jointly validated by the higher education institutions and professional bodies such as social work, psychology, physiotherapy, tended to accentuate these divisions. On the one hand, there was concern that undergraduate programmes which had assessed professional placements (2 years college based and 2 years professional training with concurrent study) were launching students into an uncritical training context where they were expected to absorb the functional roles of outside agencies and conform to these in a series of conditioned reflexes. All these expectations were allegedly taking place without any opportunity on the students' part to engage in critical analysis of various theoretical frames of reference or to examine rigorously the historical context and value assumptions in social institutions in which they were ultimately going to be practising. There were real fears that the primary goals of higher education, namely the perception of the need for clearer ideas, for a sense of perplexity and awareness of the limitations to knowledge, were being replaced by a less rigorous and even potentially unhealthy didactic approach to teaching and learning. The expository qualities of teaching were being supplanted by urgent needs to know 'how to do things'.

On the other hand, the traditional university approach had been criticized as too smug, self-contained and self-deluding. The pursuit of 'truth' and pure research for its own sake was insular and suffered from the lack of any real dialectical relationship with the outside world. Birch put the alternative case:

> The creation of a more open and interactive as well as an integrated system of higher education, which both embraces the full meaning of a broader academic ethic and demonstrates its efficiency and accountability, would raise confidence and sharpen and fulfil more certainly expectations on the part of students. Such a system would also be able to present a more convincing image to the public and to the world of affairs through achieving a stronger, mutual relationship between scholarship and society.

(W Birch 1988 p 76.)

In terms of their personal development, students gain immensely by being confronted with practical problem-solving which requires a selective use of their theoretical knowledge. This does not necessarily suggest that the work has to be uncritically undertaken – the social implications of professional actions and the mandate for agency functions should all be considered comprehensively in any practical work placement. Without doubt the process of resolving problems, finding and clarifying contradictions, confronting ethical issues, can have a profoundly formative impact and accelerate the personal growth of students.

Hence there is an undeniable necessity for all Faculties to examine ways in which practical work of whatever length or with whatever objectives, assessed or unassessed, can be built into all courses. Whether it be the more obvious area such as geography, environmental science or the apparently abstract areas such as moral philosophy or pure mathematics, opportunities can be devised at the very least for observational practice experience if not extended supervised practice.

The Principles of Independent Learning

Smith makes a number of observations about the conditions in which learning takes place (Smith 1988). Firstly learning is a lifelong process which happens intentionally or unintentionally, painfully as well as pleasurably. It is essentially a process which takes place within a person, not imposed from the outside. This process is reinforced by the person actively accepting responsibility for learning, and not behaving like a passive sponge. Inevitably learning involves change, however minute or gigantic. This very fact, especially if it means that the person will be taken into unknown territory, can provoke fear or anxiety, and even set up some form of resistance, denial or avoidance. In a sense it feels safer sometimes to remain ignorant. As the person develops emotionally and biologically, these changes affect and are affected by learning. Indeed as the individual moves from stability through transition in various ways during the life cycle, learning can constitute an important way of coping with potential upheavals. For instance, facing retirement can be a most positive challenge if the individual has prepared for it mentally as well as practically.

A necessary component of learning is that the person must interact with the environment. In this respect, experience can be both positive and inhibiting to the adult learner. It becomes an obstacle unless the learner manages to go through a real process of reorganizing and reintegrating previous experience. Otherwise what happened in the past just becomes a collection of untested prejudices. Positive reintegration can lead to acquisition of new information, skills, attitudes, understandings and values.

Independent Learning and Information Technology

The promotion of self-paced independent learning through the imaginative use of information technology is going to be increasingly significant. This is not to say that the traditional ability to 'read' a book literally will have declining priority. On the contrary it is arguable that too many third level courses pack the students' timetables so densely with transmitted material through lectures that they run the risk of stultifying the students' capacity to analyze and critically reflect. Rather it is suggested that students should have options alongside taught courses and private study, to make use of modern advances in technology to maximise their learning.

In a research project in New York in 1984 , student retention was compared in a traditional lecture-based setting to retention in three other learning environments. The first alternative setting consisted of presentation of the same content material about management studies through the medium of an interaction video disc in a classroom, with an instructor leading the discussion (one-on-many). As a second alternative (one-on-few), groups of five students worked on a copy of the same video disk material outside the classroom. Thirdly (one-on-one) individual students worked on their own personal copies of the videodisc outside the classroom. The results demonstrated significant learning gains for all the videodisc modes over the traditional lecture-based mode. (J E Vadas 1984.)

Table 1

Experimental Videodisc Module

Gaining Learning Environment Mastery	No	%
Lecture-based classroom	249	11.6
One-on-many	248	36.7
One-on-few	99	42.5
One-on-one	21	42.9
Total	617	

Interactive video users reports reveal the following findings:

I   **Increased retention.** It is asserted that people retain about 25% of what they hear, 45% of what they see and hear, and 70% of what they see, hear and do.

II   **Decreased learning time.** It is calculated that students learn material 40% faster with interactive video systems.

III   **Learner involvement.** It is a vital factor that the student actually enjoys the experience of interactive video because it is customized to specific educational needs.

IV   **Increased productivity.** By increasing the productivity of time and energy, this leads to a general increase in overall productivity.

Such evaluation suggests that if there are sound learning principles built into an interactive program, then the student may actually retain and comprehend material to a much more substantial extent than the traditional lecture will achieve.

The Need to develop Generic Learning Skills through Interactive Programs
The University of Ulster has a relatively high proportion of mature students in its population (c 30%). Some are redundant workers or long-term unemployed people seeking an alternative qualification. Others might be women whose formal education was halted because of family needs, who now wish to have a 'second chance'. One common factor among many of these students is the 'distance', both chronologically and psychologically from their last full-time educational experience. As a result, there may be difficulties in establishing a study style, uncertainty about academic expectations, and, if not fear of failure, very often an anxiety that

threatens to become crippling. This is not to say that such features are restricted to mature students. Without wishing to generalize unduly, school-leavers often enter higher education with less than ideal preparation. The transition from descriptive regurgitation to critical analysis can be painful. Indeed the very invitation to express an opinion can be actually anxiety-arousing. Sometimes the secondary school experience has even been damaging in the sense that unconventionality has been punished as out of place with a subsequent loss of confidence on the part of the pupil.

Thus, in the context of 35-40% of Ulster's school-leavers entering higher education by the end of the decade, priority has to be given to making available to the students, as a precursor to academic study, the opportunity to develop sound generic learning skills – the tools to apply to their own chosen discipline.

Entwhistle (1992) points to recent research revealing general student dissatisfaction with the help provided in higher education to develop appropriate study skills. Furthermore he quotes several studies which indicate that the lack of comprehensive study skills support is one of the reasons for either drop-out or eventual academic failure.

Of course counsellors in the British and Irish universities have been leading study skills workshops for many years. The traditional themes have included:

> reading books effectively;
> taking notes in lectures;
> developing a framework for essays;
> revision methods;
> examination techniques;
> relaxation techniques.

Most counsellors adopt the strategy of starting where the group members are in terms of their stage of learning, their immediate concerns, and the tasks that they wish to work on. The group members actually compile their own agenda, and are usually encouraged to use each other as valuable resources. As a result, the participants come to recognize the common ground that they share, and if they develop a strong mutual trust, the group can move to a very profound level of examination of attitudes to learning. It can also be the case that some members of the group are also seeing the counsellor on an individual basis because of personal dimensions to difficulties that are not appropriate to this type of group context.

Undoubtedly this form of counsellor-led dialogical approach to learning (and basic confidence-building) will remain a key part of the support services to students.

The University of Ulster Hypertext Project

To supplement the professional resources of the counselling team, and the Faculty studies advisers, the Principal Computing Officer at the University of Ulster and the author decided to try to construct an interactive hypertext-based program on study skills. Hypertext was chosen because of its graphics capabilities, as a fundamental prerequisite was the engagement and participation of the student learner. Basic text was readily available from a wide range of educational manuals and study guides, and hand-outs which the University counsellors had generated through their practice experience. For the first volume the areas of revision and essay-writing were considered. Volume 2 addresses examination technique. Key principles in deciding how to organize and illustrate the material included the following:

(i) avoidance of lengthy boring text;

(ii) use of relevant visual imagery;

(iii) opportunities for the student to identify *personal* issues or concerns to work on;

(iv) pay-off for students' efforts in the form of print-outs of personal material;

(v) scoring systems, and opportunities to recapitulate to reinforce learning;

(vi) encouragement of insight learning – eg how to construct a 'key word' card which summarizes concepts;

(vii) evaluation of the program in terms of its usefulness – ie the student is invited to contribute to future students by suggesting improvements.

As to potential usage, each program is flexible in that it can be used;

(a) by the student alone at a PC;

(b) in combination with tutorial work with a tutor;

(c) alongside or parallel to contact with a counsellor;

(d) in a peer support group context.

Workstations or individual Apple Mac PCs could be made available in a wide range of locations: libraries, waiting areas, study bedrooms in Halls, computer laboratories, Faculty common rooms, students' lodgings.

The basic objective of these programs is to help the students develop the skills of independent learning which can be utilized in any discipline and which are an essential complement to taught courses.

The Need for an Integrated Approach

Where students have special needs arising from specific learning difficulties (eg dyslexia), physical disability or socio-economic background, all universities should, by dint of their central support services, have the in-built capacity for:

(a) assessment of special needs;

(b) compilation of a support programme (including any special examination arrangements to meet those specific needs;

(c) availability of specialized equipment and computer hardware and software (eg talk-back computer programs, print enlargement, electronic braille).

The author had the privilege of visiting several universities in the state and private sector in California in January 1992, and was impressed by the commitment shown to 'affirmative action programs'. Often Learning Development Units were provided in a very cost-effective way (including assessment expertise) which served the Faculties and ensure that all students were given real equality of opportunity to achieve this maximum academic potential. It would be an unforgivable dereliction of duty if the British and Irish universities paid lip-service to widening access to disadvantaged or disabled people but in reality left them to 'sink or swim'. At the University of Ulster, efforts are being made to meet these responsibilities by widening the scope of the counselling team to include an educational psychologist and a guidance officer whose brief will be to support students with special needs arising from disability or socio-economic background.

Student Peer Support

Another prominent feature of the Californian university system was the encouragement of student peer support. This related to both the academic and the social welfare spheres. It is this author's view that, as long as schemes do not replace professional jobs 'on the cheap', there is great scope and potency in the employment of student peers. This may consist of senior students volunteering to help orientate new arrivals into their own discipline area; students interested in cross-cultural experience or language development 'pairing' with international students for a combination of social and educational purposes. The University of California at Davis had a particularly fine example of social welfare support provided by students for students in a detached house allotted on the campus. A 24-hour service was maintained to enable students in social or emotional crisis to 'drop in' with or without appointment. Supported by a senior counsellor on the organizing committee, the students rigorously trained their new volunteers in a comprehensive course lasting several weeks. Clearly such schemes should only be made available as voluntary options, complementary to the professional academic and support services. However the tantalizing fact of the matter is that often the student may learn as much if not more from peer interaction than the more formalized contacts with university staff.

(b) The Personal Development of Students

The concept 'personal development' is used here in an all-embracing way, relating to the intellectual, social, emotional and cultural maturation of the student. While the experience of higher education is by its very nature a transient one, it has potentially a highly significant influence at a key stage of people's lives. Therefore it is not too grandiose to claim that profound advances may be made by a student, not just at a cognitive level, but in terms of the wider sensibilities. Attitudes and long-held assumptions may be altered or challenged; new forms of stimulation through social interaction with people of different backgrounds and ideas may cause a re-appraisal of the person's own value system; the young adult may be directly or indirectly assisted in the difficult passage from late adolescence towards at least the shaping of a personal identity that has some coherence; the 'second chance' mature student may be enabled to overcome emotional blockages to earlier learning and develop an enhanced self-esteem through academic achievement; or the graduate may discover even more about personal potential by pursuing a research degree.

If the student is able to experience the intellectual culture of academic life in a comprehensive way, the manifest outcome is a more integrated personality, more secure in his or her strengths and qualities, able to acknowledge the uncertainty of knowledge with tolerance and humility, and ready to play an active role in whatever chosen field in the outside world.

In describing a similar state of being, Bassey borrows the concept from Ivan Illich of 'conviviality':

> Conviviality has a profound meaning concerned with the nature of human life. ... A convivial person is trying to evolve a state of deep and satisfying harmony with the world, which gives joyful meaning to life. Convivial people are striving for harmony with their environment, with their fellows and with their self. (M Bassey 1987 p 12.)

Generic Needs at Entry into University.

Students of whatever age who make the decision to enter higher education bring with them the same broad range of common human needs, and it is imperative that a network of services is available to assist when appropriate so that initial adjustments can be made satisfactorily.

Nurturance:

Self-evidently adequate food and drink are primary needs which are at the apex of the hierarchy of basic human needs. Bearing in mind that the considerable majority of new entrants are in the age range 18-19 years there can be no automatic assumption that they have either the skills or the knowledge to prepare a regimen of nutritious meals which are both economical and appetizing. And over the years evidence has accumulated to demonstrate that competence in domestic science is not determined by the gender of the student. Some of the most alarming examples of lack of proper sustenance have concerned female students who, perhaps related to other adjustment issues to do with self-image, have been discovered to be barely surviving on starvation diets. In contrast an average 18 year old male may not usually prepare a great array of meals but will fill up an empty stomach with readily available glutinous carbohydrates.

The significance of a proper nutritious diet is immense in that it helps to guarantee a general sense of wellbeing and assists the student in coping with the range of demands that the new environment brings. Proteins and vitamins literally energize the individual whereas undernourishment dulls the senses.

Indubitably the economic situation of the student is also very germane. A meagre diet of rice and pasta may well be linked to the poverty-stricken predicament of the student, albeit a short-term one. Hence there is a cogent argument that either the Students' Union or the Student Services Department should provide a freely available information booklet, containing advice about the best sources of nutrition and fibre in food, and actual recipes which are going to be within the financial means of the great majority. Most universities have departments within their Science, Technology or Health and Social Sciences Faculties whose expertise could be brought to bear on such a project at little expense.

With regard to all the support services, it is critically important that the institution does not lapse into paternalistic postures on the misplaced assumption that it is 'in loco parentis'. All students entering higher education are adults, even if many are intellectually and emotionally in a state of formative flux. The most valid role that the college can play is to make sound and accurate information available in a non-judgemental fashion and leave it to the student to think through the consequences of any personal actions. Accepting responsibility for your own actions is an intrinsic element in becoming a capable and functioning individual.

An area in which this tenet is truly put to the test is the question of the consumption of alcohol. All third level campuses provide easy access to alcohol and, indeed, through commercial sponsorship, there are poetically dubbed phenomena known as 'Happy Hours' when the price of a drink is at least halved! The thrust behind these initiatives appears to be a combination of inducing a campus community spirit and touting the merits of the latest brands of 'aqua vitae'!

Be that as it may, the student entering the university has an immediately available option to use the bar to a lesser or greater extent as a forum for conviviality. Depending on the sub-cultural ethos, the imbibing of alcohol will be linked in varying degrees to social intercourse and the formation of new friendships. For many school-leavers it will also be the location for the very first experimentation with alcohol away from the scrutiny of parents, school teachers or clergy. Objectively, the information booklets may indicate to the students that alcohol is a pleasant and useful social drug if contained within moderate bounds – the most common mathematical formula being not more than three 'units' of alcohol on not more than three occasions per week. Notwithstanding the student may still learn about the impact of abuse of alcohol by the trial and error methods of egestion and regurgitation!

Given the importance of maintaining a reasonable diet on a low income, the educational establishment will always have a standing obligation to provide a subsidized refectory service of good quality. Without indulging in moralizing paternalism, it should also make available non-alcoholic common rooms for refreshment and socializing.

Shelter:

Another primary need which has both physical and emotional connotations is that for shelter. Most students who arrive on the campus, whatever their age or social background, will have come from some form of residential arrangement which has kept the weather out and provided at least minimum warmth and security. The school-leaver will normally have had cossetted dependency status in the parental home. Perhaps the mature student has been a partner in acquiring a family home, and is either travelling to college from that home or joining the ranks of the school-leavers in seeking term-time accommodation. A minority of students will be travelling from various life-styles overseas and another small sub-set with special needs arising from ill-health or disability may be arriving from residential settings such as hospitals or boarding schools.

Finding a new niche comprising ingredients which suit the particular lifestyle of the student is an anxiety-provoking task, the import of which on the whole transition into academic life cannot be underestimated. 'Shelter' denotes a much wider need than mere physical roof over the head. It signifies the human need for respite and privacy; the opportunity to withdraw into a personal environment of one's own choosing. It will be the location in which much of the essentially solitary task of reading and scholarly writing will be enacted, with the inherent implication that it must be at least tolerably warm and congenial. Unless the student has an arrangement in Student Residences whereby all meals are provided, the new accommodation will be the place where the existent or acquired skills in self-catering are implemented. It will also establish the pattern for much of the informal social interaction that the student experiences outside formal course attendance on campus.

Acceptance and Belonging:

In terms of the psychology of adjustment to a new milieu, a healthy and positive transition will only take place if the primary needs for acceptance and a sense of belonging are satiated. Working definitions of terms are probably helpful here. 'Acceptance' is experienced by an individual cognitively and emotionally if the signals from the environment are ones of respect and according of rights as a fellow human being, regardless of the socio-economic, cultural or racial background of the individual. 'A sense of belonging', it is suggested, is only accomplished when the newcomer feels that either there is extensive common ground in terms of values and aspirations or that the encumbent group has shown evidence of novel values and ideas which the new arrival finds attractive and into which in time he or she wishes to be incorporated. Both states of being if accomplished constitute a perspective of trust in immediate peers and leaders; and hopeful confidence that the work completed together will be worthwhile, even if challenging, and will lead to mutually desired goals. Conversely if neither of these states is achieved, the behaviour likely to emanate will be highly conservative, conformist and distrustful if not altogether alienated.

A central and recurring thesis in this work is that students need to feel accepted and develop a sense of belonging to the intellectual culture of a campus in order that their energies and creative imaginations may be released; in order that they will be free and courageous enough to face challenges and take risks; and in order that they will even come to challenge and criticize some of the assumed knowledge promulgated by their academic mentors. How is the attitudinal and spiritual ethos established and signalled that achieves such an uplifting impact on the student?

At the outset it is useful to discuss some features of group activity which would totally negate any process of acceptance and sense of belonging. Lewis, in a survey of student attitudes, issues a word of caution about the dangers if it is not appreciated that an academic course represents a temporary short-term experience for a student:

> It seems that it is a feature of the student experience to find groups of like-minded others – whether through social or academic contacts – and, eventually, become more inward than outward looking. Perhaps the

> recognition of the essentially transient nature of the university experience
> for students enhances this development.   (I Lewis 1984 p 139.)

He jangles the nerve-ends of well-meaning administrators by asserting that this form of defensive and conservative sub-grouping may in fact be the direct consequence of official interventions that are meant to be helpful forms of induction! The basic source of this dissonance stems from the fact that students in actuality are transient people who embody with each cohort perpetually changing values and needs. Consequently the students themselves have historically specific perceptions of their own needs. These may not, in fact probably will not, match up with the perceptions of the Provost as he or she steps up to deliver the traditional Freshers' address or the senior tutor whose conception of what it must be like to arrive in this strange place dates back twenty years.

Highly organized induction programmes may also serve to heighten and not diminish the anxiety of the new students. By early detailed discussion of issues such as adjustment to higher education study styles, time management priorities, perambulations concerning deadlines in intermittent assessment, the course tutors may in reality be highlighting the complexity of the transition that the students are undergoing and reinforcing in them their instinct to dash into a familiar sub-group for safety!

> An immediate requirement therefore must be that academic staff take pains
> to find out about the dimensions of the world which students inhabit, the
> pressures they feel, the competing demands made of them. This cannot be
> done by relying solely upon a contrived mechanism of supervision, with
> institutional procedures and relatively sparse contacts.   (I. Lewis, 1984.)

If the students' perceptions are not honestly checked out, corrosive doubts can occur in relation to academic studies; students can and do develop perceptions about 'hidden curriculum' mixed messages within their Faculties. On the one hand they hear stirring speeches about the benefits of adventurous and imaginative exploration in their thinking; then they receive jarring antidotes that strongly suggest that third level study is primarily geared to deadlines, and reproducing narrowly constructed knowledge to achieve pass marks in examinations:

> ...we found evidence of the distance between staff and students reflected in
> the student perceptions of staff as authorities, both of their subject specialisms
> and also of the grading of student work. The immediate consequence was
> that, in spite of staff intentions to provide opportunities for students to begin
> to do small-scale original and independent work, students operated
> predominantly within the guidelines they took from preliminary booklets.

> By demonstrating a lack of originality and independence they confirm the
> faculty perspective that students are not really capable of such activities.'
>
> (I. Lewis, 1984.)

In order to ensure that potentially lively and creative students are not entrapped by syllabus content and assessment deadlines, the course teaching team must continuously review the objectives of their courses and the style of assessment. And tutors need to tune in as fully as possible to the fact that students are complex multifaceted organisms who, in order to develop and enrich themselves, need to have the space to allow other demands on their time without guilt or anxiety about failing to meet the expectations of the course. Is it possible that a lack of critical reappraisal of course content and assessment criteria can in itself create the conflicts in time management for which students are then blamed?

Ultimately the student's sense of belonging will hinge on the closeness of the identification with the immediate peer group and the specific academic department. It will be nurtured informally by the invigorating discovery that new friends do share common interests and value the student as a companion. Accompanying the growing sense of belonging will be a growing sureness about why the student has chosen this route. Truscot advocated that, periodically students should have the opportunity to spend short periods in residence in extra mural houses with their academic tutors and professors in order to engage in more personalized dialogue and be invigorated by the enthusiasm of the staff for their subjects; even inspired by autobiographical accounts illustrating how their mentors developed their love for their work. (B Truscot 1951). This vision of a shared spirituality is surely one that has timeless relevance?

Self-actualization:

In common with fellow human beings, students have a primary need to organize a coherent set of values that have meaning, and to work out directions and pathways in which they can release their energies in a purposeful way. During their academic careers they are literally living through psychosocial stage of development towards what Erikson termed the ultimate stage of 'wisdom' when the blended qualities of cognition, emotion and intuition coalesce. (Erikson 1963).

Maslow identifies the key features of self-actualization as:

- a form of selflessness, wherein the person comes to experience vividly, with full concentration and absorption, and without negative defences;

- a continual process which has elements of progress and regression, being honest or cheating, stealing or not stealing; growth choices or fear choices;

- a preparedness to listen to the 'impulse' voice of the self and give an honest opinion as opposed to a bogus acquiescent one;

- opting to be courageous rather than afraid of unpopularity;

- being prepared no matter how arduous the process to give an outlet to potential abilities;

- having peak experiences, literally ecstatic moments, which are transient instance of self-actualization – these are surprises which cannot be guaranteed or bought but the hard groundwork has to be done by the individual to produce these 'peaks';

- insight into one's limitations as well as potentialities; the giving up of restrictive defences such as repression; this can be anxiety-provoking and uncomfortable but necessary.

Self-actualization is in practice not a matter of one great moment but is a matter of degree. Little gains or accessions are achieved one by one, putting the individuals in touch with their own biological natures, and their congenital inheritance.

The ultimate result of self-actualization is that the person becomes as full a human being as possible, reaching some form of state of insight and truth. (A H Maslow 1971).

Even with the widening of access to higher education since the 1960s, students are still in a relatively privileged position to work out career paths and realize personal potential. Notwithstanding there are various structural obstacles which threaten to slow or derail this momentum, and with which, in its role as a facilitating agent, the academic institution must be careful not to collude. An immense and insidious example of such barriers is the influence of stereotyping. On the campus, the negative consequences of this form of block treatment of human beings can be witnessed in two sub-groups of the student population – women and overseas students.

(i) **Women and Socialization**: Because of the residual attitudes in wider society about 'appropriate' behaviours within sexual roles, it is evident that more female students proportionately still tend to opt for Arts and Social Sciences courses in higher education. In a study of females in a minority situation on a science course, Thomas commented that:

> The female physics students experienced difficulty in coping with the new environment — this is as a direct result of the attitudes of staff and fellow students towards them. In particular there was difficulty in reconciling the notions of 'femininity' and 'physicist', as Physics is perceived, rightly or

wrongly, as requiring peculiarly 'male' or masculine qualities. The women are treated as a 'minority group' and because of this, they, too, perceive themselves collectively, in opposition to the competitive and individualistic environment of the department. The male arts students on the other hand, did not experience this treatment and tended to regard themselves as individuals:

...the formative experiences of the first year result in many female physics students feeling inadequate and unable to cope, whilst there appears to be no such adverse effects for male English students.

... there needs to be a much greater flexibility and tolerance in subjects such as Physics and the existing divides between 'cultural' and 'vocational', 'instrumental' and 'expressive' disciplines need to be bridged for the benefit of both male and female students.

(K Thomas 1986 p 25.)

Delamont suggests that models for male-female relations which predominate among academic staff themselves are all potentially antithetical to open and egalitarian professional relationships between male and female colleagues. She describes these as; kinship (father-daughter), marriage, romance (female status equalling wife, girlfriend, or mistress), quasi-scientific roles (woman scientist perceived as lab technician or assistant.) And because scientific research has its own indeterminacy, technicality and 'habitus', it is extremely difficult for women to penetrate this scholarly world at a high level. She concludes that:

The argument of this section, which can be made about other professional occupations such as law, medicine and architecture as well as science, is that women's failure to be accepted as full members of the occupation is due to the fact that many aspects of the occupation's 'habitus', especially the indeterminate aspects of job performance, are hidden from a substantial proportion of the members, including the women and the ethnic minorities, by Saturn's Rings. (S Delamont 1989 p 261.)

It would appear that some Faculties, especially in fields such as Science, Medicine, Law and Engineering need to re-examine candidly the extent to which their own conditioned suppositions about sex-roles and their professional exclusiveness have corporately combined to discriminate against the just advancement of women and, in turn, have reinforced the lack of confidence that women feel in pursuing such professional routes. The proportional imbalances in choice of undergraduate courses are vividly illustrated in the following Table.

Table B
Full-time Undergraduates at United Kingdom Universities
by Subject Group of Study 1987–88

Subject Group of Study

	Total	Men	Women
1. Medicine and Dentistry	23,673	13,106	10,567
2. Studies allied to Medicine	7,351	2,269	5,082
3. Biological Sciences	17,568	7,856	9,712
4. Veterinary Sciences, Agriculture and related studies	4,928	2,650	2,278
5. Physical Sciences	20,546	15,095	5,451
6. Mathematical Sciences	16,074	12,063	4,011
7. Engineering & Technology	34,236	30,683	3,553
8. Architecture and related studies	4,311	3,101	1,210
9. Social Sciences	37,848	19,897	17,951
10. Business and financial studies	12,440	7,096	5,344
11. Librarianship and Information Science	427	126	301
12. Languages and related studies	28,268	8,276	19,992
13. Humanities	15,741	8,375	7,366
14. Creative Arts	4,290	1,687	7,366
15. Education	2,886	752	2,134
16. Multi-disciplinary Studies	34,216	17,776	16,440

(Source: UGC University Statistics 1987-88 Vol 1 Students and Staff Universities' Statistical Record pps 14 and 15.)

(ii) **The Stereotyping of Overseas Students**: Of all social systems in our society, universities are normally perceived as international meeting places where enriching cross-fertilization of many cultures is a 'sine qua non'. Worryingly, Lewis's attitudinal survey indicates that, as a direct consequence of English being a second language for most overseas students, there may be misplaced and stereotypic assessments expounded by lecturers when academic difficulties occur. In particular there may be an automatic and facile interpretation that apparent lack of command of spoken English is the central problem when this might not be the case. Difficulties may be more related to the transitional stresses of entering an entirely new cultural milieu perhaps even exacerbated by insensitive institutional practice:

> Given the earlier evidence concerning the interrelationship between the academic and social dimensions of the student world, it might not be surprising that a group of students, who experience a substantial range of problems of adjustment to a strange set of social circumstances, also

experience some academic difficulties. If English is not their first language, and if the main focus of the staff perspective is a concern for academic performance, then conceivably, academic difficulties can easily be seen to stem from language problems. A symptom of the difficulty of social integration becomes transmuted into a cause of academic difficulties.

(I Lewis 1984 p 140).

Chapter Five

An Ideal-Type Model of Student Support Services

It is a basic tenet of this book that, in order to maximize the benefit that students derive from their stay in the university, they may from time to time need to seek out the advice and assistance of various support services. This chapter will attempt to identify in ideal-type form the principles and objectives which should underpin such services. However it must be emphasized that, far from there being a consensus about the need for such services in depth, a wide variety of views exist on this issue among academic and administrative staff. These are best illustrated in the form of the following typology of attitudes.

(a) The 'Sink or Swim' School
The adherents to this school of thought tend to regard themselves as 'self-made' people. They attribute the success which they have achieved in their careers to their ability to summon forth inner resources during difficult times in their lives. Indeed they would see it as part of character development to survive and grow against the odds. The basic values reflected in this position are the perfect constituents for the Friedman economist or the Newtonian disciple who actually believes in the survival of the fittest. This school firmly believes that support services in universities tend to mollycoddle students and encourage unhealthy dependency.

(b) The 'Laissez-faire' School
This school tends to be comprised of social scientists with a leaning towards Marxian philosophy. Basically this group has a rather sceptical view of the educational system in general, believing it to be an active agent of social control and conditioning even at the third level. Hence their basic stance in relation to students is one of 'radical non-intervention'. In practice, as studies advisers, such people might demonstrate great empathy towards students if approached by them, but would probably never arrange a structured interview as a matter of principle.

(c) The 'In Loco Parentis' School
These are the traditionalists of the higher education system, long in the tooth,

worldly-wise, who believe that they have been given a mandate by society to provide a structured experience for young people. In pedagogical terms they tend to see education as a transmission of knowledge with the students being empty vessels to be filled and in social terms they see their role as instilling the values of good citizenship into the young. They would therefore encourage the development of student support services, but would tend to define the role of such services in a prescriptive and structured way. Some of the most obvious examples of adherence to this school of thought are in the form of senior administrators who, if they ever taught students at all, have long since ceased to have direct contact with them. This social distance tends to be reflected in a basic lack of trust of young people and the desire to keep them under very strict control.

(d) The 'Adult to Adult' School

The proponents of this school are open to caricature as the remnants of the Liberal tradition. They actually believe that from the age of eighteen young people should be treated literally as adults and encouraged to take full responsibility for their own learning and existence. Like all human beings, the students will need from time to time the temporary support of a significant person in their lives to help them overcome a crisis or setback. However essentially students are regarded as people who carry with them into the higher education substantial resources in terms of their intelligence, skills and experience. Indeed they may from time to time teach the tutor as well as being the subjects of the learning process. The emphasis in this model is on active participation and encouragement to make decisions and to take risks.

Consequently the academic institution far from reflecting consensus views about the personal development of students, is a complex social system with a wide variety of value positions, biases and prejudices. By the same token there is no uniform structure to the student support services themselves within the institutions. Many of the services have structures peculiarly linked to their particular historical context in their own institutions. For instance some have a long tradition of employing full-time medical officers and nursing staff on campus, providing services not just for students but geared to the occupational health of the staff as well. In others general practitioners are invited onto the campus, perhaps alongside dental surgeons, to provide sessional health care and are paid pro rata fees for their services. Others simply rely on the fail-safe net of the National Health Service and expect all students simply to register with health centres in the immediate community. This latter option holds a certain obvious economic attraction to administrators who are concerned about cutting expenditure, but also reveals a lack of belief in the importance of a residential collegiate spirit.

With the growth of institution-owned student residences between the 1950s and the 1970s, and the rising need for off-campus accommodation due to increasing student numbers, most universities have some form of accommodation service on campus. However the practitioners may be on the staff of the Building and Estates Department or the Secretary's Department and consequently may not have a well developed or discrete professional identity. In the absence of a coherent training course specifically geared towards the needs of housing management in education, many of these staff are 'sub-professional' both in their conditions of service and their outlook. On the other hand some accommodation officers who have been given a distinct identity have been able to initiate highly imaginative accommodation projects and provide very comprehensive advisory services for their students.

The role of counsellors is a relatively recent one, having risen to prominence only from the late 1960s onwards. This coincided with the increase in specially devised post-graduate training courses in counselling throughout Britain. The current situation is that the majority of counsellors have some form of professional qualification, be it specifically in counselling or in a related area such as social work, probation, psychotherapy or psychiatry. At the same time there are a substantial number of counsellors who have a much broader welfare role providing more of an information-giving service rather than one of skilled intervention. Within the last decade there has been growing evidence that universities have had more and more of a felt need for counselling services. A generally accepted view is that, with the increased competitiveness in the third level sector and the growing concern about availability of suitable jobs, the stress level in both the undergraduate and the postgraduate student populations has been noticeably rising.

Crises of motivation, reactive depressions, and other severe mental health problems feature in varying degrees in all institutions and sensible academic and administrative staff realize the need for professional expertise on the campus.

With regard to the careers service, this sector of activities has professionalized to a considerable extent in the last few years. Coinciding with the expansionist vision of the Robbins Report, the Heyworth Report on University Appointments Boards was published in 1965. This report defined the purpose of an oppointments/careers service in a way that has changed little in the succeeding twenty years:

> The business of the Appointments Boards, then, is to help the new graduate across the gap between the last lecture and the first job, bearing in mind both the needs and abilities of the individual graduate and the just demands of society upon him as expressed in the kind of employment he is asked to undertake. (Heyworth Report 1964 p 4.)

At that time there were three main elements to the appointments service:

advisory interviews between appointments/careers officers and students; an information service about career routes, current job vacancies and specific employers; and circulation of vacancy bulletins and arrangement of individual interviews between students and employers. The appointments officers came from a variety of backgrounds such as personnel management, youth employment services, commerce and teaching. There was no uniform qualification, and interviewing skills and 'emotional and physical toughness' were regarded as the primary qualities required. (Ibid p 10).

The Heyworth Report concluded that the increase in the student numbers in higher education had not been matched by the resources of the appointments services which ranged from "barely adequate to frankly rudimentary". (Ibid p 87).

With the arrival of modern information technology, the databases and access to communication networks have become much more sophisticated. Many careers officers are now trained and skilled in vocational guidance and counselling practice; and professional development of the service has been facilitated by the very active and progressive Association of Graduate Careers Advisory Services.

The modern international perspective of both the careers and counselling services is reflected in their participation in 'FEDORA', an association recently formed to promote exchange of information and advice about opportunities for study and work in the European community; and to disseminate the results of studies and research.

An Integrated Model of Academic and Support Services
It has been argued throughout this book that universities should provide opportunities in a holistic way for the personal development of students. The transformation which the students can potentially experience refers to social, emotional and cultural growth as well as intellectual advancement. If recent political prophesies are accurate, there will be not only a considerable increase in the overall student population by the end of the century, but the nature of that population will be immensely more heterogeneous, both in terms of age groups and social and cultural backgrounds. To maximize the potential benefit of the students' transitory sojourns on campus, there must be an integrated approach to the provision of academic and support services, both vertically in terms of a facilitating management ethos and horizontally in the sense of close co-operation and shared objectives between academic and administrative personnel.

The guiding principles which must underpin the administration of support services, if personal development of students is to be truly facilitated, include the following:

1. Compatible and complementary services should be contained within the umbrella of one department, the Student Services, so that they can be identified easily and clearly by the students.

2. Sources of advice, guidance and support should be physically accessible as opposed to being camouflaged from the public view.

3. Personal support services for students must be provided in ways that are not stigmatizing. They should be openly and universally available to all students (and staff).

4. Those professional services which involve confidential and private matters concerning the students must be visibly independent from the academic departments and other non- personal administrative departments.

5. Because of the depth of skill and knowledge required, and the interpersonal nature of the work, the officers employed in personal support services should preferably have relevant professional qualifications and participate regularly in staff development courses and in-service training.

6. These professional officers should have the capacity to think and work as integrated interdisciplinary teams because of the inevitable common ground and overlap in the services.

7. Personal support services must always be made available on a purely optional and voluntary basis.

8. As well as catering for the needs of students as individuals on campus, Student Services should also be made accessible to other significant persons in the lives of the students if this is deemed appropriate eg spouses, parents, children, friends.

9. The ethos of the personal student services must always be concerned with working with students as self-determining adults; it is not appropriate to foster dependency in students on the erroneous basis that the university acts 'in loco parentis'.

10. In all aspects of the students' personal and social life on campus, the students' right to privacy and personal choice must be safeguarded.

11. As a personalised and private service, the Student Services must act in a relatively autonomous professional manner but should show accountability by reporting in general terms to an appropriate central committee on its activities.

12. There should be regular liaison and cross-referral between the Student Services and the academic tutors concerning the welfare of the students. No information should normally be exchanged, however, without the explicit consent of the students concerned.

The Administrative Structure of the Student Services

The Student Services should incorporate under one administrative umbrella the following essential services:

(i) Accommodation Officers and ancillary staff addressing both on-campus and off-campus accommodation needs.

(ii) Health Personnel: because of the special needs of students living away from home and the desirability of rapid access, each Student Services team should include full-time nursing staff and either salaried or sessionally employed medical officers.

(iii) Counsellors: these staff should be professionally qualified to undertake both individual work with students and social groupwork, eg study skills groups, mature student groups.

(iv) Careers advisory officers: in this model, it is essential to have careers advisory officers as part of a universal service. It is not acceptable that such personnel should gear their activities solely or primarily to the external needs of the free-floating market economy. Rather they should be non-judgemental facilitators enabling students to weigh up options in career choices without the interference of vested interests.

(v) Child-minding staff; it should fall to the Student Services to provide, as an essential and not just a desirable facility, a fully equipped and professionally staffed nursery playgroup.

(vi) General welfare staff: such personnel should be available who can assist sensitively and empathically with important administrative and practical matters such as collection of residential fees; the implementation of loan schemes in cases of financial crisis or hardship; support for students with special needs arising from disability.

In broad outline, then, these are the professional officers who are required as a minimum essential by all universities if they are to be able to claim honestly that they are concerned about the broader personal development of their students. What are the more detailed activities and initiatives that should be taking place, consistent with the guiding principles already outlined? For the sake of clarity, the main professional areas will be addressed in turn, although in reality the boundaries are much more fluid and interconnected.

1. Accommodation

Choice of suitable accommodation based on a clear knowledge of options and their implications is one of the key decisions to be taken by the student, and this usually occurs before the teaching term commences. With regard to the accommodation services provided by the institution, there are several imperatives which arise from this primary need of students.

(i) As an integrated element within the academic plan of the institution, there must be a rigorous estimation of the proportion of students who will in future years be living away from their own homes. In close conjunction with these projected target figures, the Student Services should devise a comprehensive accommodation plan which takes into account all the local factors which are relevant. This accommodation plan should identify realistically the number of student bed-places which will be available in the following sectors:

(a) **Institution-Owned Property**. As a matter of policy, the institution should purchase, lease or build Student Residences, houses and flats within easy access of the campus. Given the fact that first year students are arriving at an unknown environment and may be indeed living away from home for the first time in their lives, there is a strong argument that the college itself should provide at least 50% of the bedplaces required for first year students, either on a self-catering basis or with a partial or full meals service. It is appreciated that since the mid 1970s there has been no capital funding made available for student housing through the University Funding Council, but there are various financial packages which can be mounted with the goodwill of the Finance Officer. Settling into satisfactory accommodation has such profound importance for the new student in terms of the overall adjustment to academic life, that such provision must rank among the highest priorities.

The exact proportion of bed places which should be owned and managed by the itself really depends on the existing provision and future possibilities within the 'hinterland' of the campus. Other essential elements in the network include:

(b) **Housing Associations**. Specialist housing associations catering for single homeless people receive capital and recurrent funding from the Government and can regard students technically as priority applicants. While requiring a separate identity and autonomy in relation to design features and location of their developments, the housing associations are normally willing to co-operate fully with the authorities of the institution in relating to siting of new provision, mutual referral and allocation policies. Some of these associations are even managed by officers from the Students Unions of local further and higher education colleges.

(c) **Public Housing**. Officials from public housing authorities are usually very willing to make lease arrangements for individual houses or flats with the Student Services Department. Indeed, where tenancy reallocation has proved slow in some estates it has been known that entire streets of houses have been made available.

(d) **Private Sector.** Either through estate agents or directly through landlords and landladies there will always be a rich vein of houses, flats and lodgings in various combinations – for instance with or without landlord present, with or without meals provided. The rents charged for these facilities tend to settle within a band which partly reflects the fees of institution-owned Residences and therefore are not normally exploitative. However, standards can vary tremendously and consequently it is critically essential that the professional officers of the Student Services keep a regularly updated register of private off-campus accommodation which is actually visited at least twice in each academic year to ensure that standards are adequate. Details can then be kept on the register of the facilities being offered for the rent and advice can be given to the incoming student.

(ii) The Student Services must also be geared to provide a personalized and accessible reception for the new students. Having secured a place on an academic course, the newcomer's first contact with officials of the institution may in fact be with the professional officers administering the accommodation service. Informative and clear explanations and demonstrating a genuine 'listening ear' are two central skills which are required. What facilities are provided in the Student Residences? How does one get around a strange new town to find the recommended landladies? (A compact photocopy of a local map is an absolute requirement as a first gift of friendship to the new student!)

Bearing in mind that all new entrants have their own background lives, relationships and former roles from which they are emerging, it establishes an immediate climate of supportive warmth if they feel they have the space to sit and talk to a willing listener even about some of their doubts and fears. It is never justifiable to hand a new student abruptly a laundry list of addresses using the rationalisation that there is no time to waste on mere talking! If the novitiate is to reorientate effectively and settle down enjoyably to a new life-style, the early contact with the accommodation officers and the extent of informative support will be vital factors.

An emphasis has been placed in this section on the responsibility of the college to provide a substantial proportion of on-campus accommodation. This practical proposal is one tangible reflection of the philosophy of the entire treatise which argues for an intellectual culture developing within the campus itself. A university should have an exciting atmosphere arising from an 'esprit de corps'; for this to be manifested to the full, the perpetual residential presence of a high proportion of the students in and around the campus will always be an essential element. This is not to say that student life should be insular and removed from the wider community – other sections of this book illustrate how integration with the world outside is another fruitful ingredient for profound personal development. Neither does this reflect a lack of recognition that, in the future, a growing proportion of students may be home-based, ensuing from financial necessity or chosen mode of study. Rather it is stressing the fact that the students 'en masse' must identify closely with their own campus in order to inject into it a climate of dynamism and creativity – an academic elan. Without their energy, the campus is a mere shell.

Emphasis on the case for baseline professional qualifications for accommodation officers is important here. This is a drastically underrated area of activity in the eyes of other academic and administrative staff and there is a compelling argument for elevating the status of the work. A simple solution to this shortcoming is in the hands of the institutions themselves in that they could mount postgraduate diploma or Masters courses specifically geared to professional training in the sphere of educational housing management.

2. Health

There is a wide range of opportunities within the health service component of Student Services to promote personal development and at the same time positively affect academic achievements. Once again, when handled with sensitive professional expertise, dangers of paternalism can be successfully avoided. In terms of their day to day physical state of health, most students are in fact disgustingly healthy and vigorous! Reviews of the statistics would indicate a range of seasonally related minor problems which reflect the run of the mill setbacks of the average citizen. However there are two broad areas where availability and timely involvement of the nurse or the doctor can be momentous and of long term significance – these can be categorized as (a) special needs and (b) health promotion.

(a) Special Needs

Disability. There is a vast and problematic educational issue which does not get the priority or attention that it merits, and in which the universities only play a relatively small but vital part. That is the issue of the lack of social justice which appears to be accorded to many physically disabled students who have the intellectual ability to proceed to the third level. Unfortunately there are very deeply interred causes for the limited horizons which seem to be the lot of many disabled students and some of these faults are embodied in the school system. The message which is often transmitted to the child is that there are too many practical obstacles in the way to permit anything but modest educational ambitions. Indeed there are such obstacles, both at a physical level in terms of access or availability of specialized information technology, and at the level of attitudes ("Why should 'able-bodied' students suffer to give positive discrimination to a small minority of disabled students at a time when resources are at a premium?") However some universities do now provide specialized facilities in their Residences and most have a much better awareness of the necessity to improve physical access to build in such considerations in new buildings. Realistically, however, what most universities have to limit their initiatives to is a form of smoothing of the path through an academic career when an individual disabled student applies and shows the academic potential. In this respect the medical staff can become involved in various helpful ways. Before the student confirms the decision to accept the place, an individualized assessment of the degree of mobility and often special needs, for instance for ongoing medical treatment, can be carried out by the health team. Thus assessment can be shared with the student who can then make a personal decision whether to attempt to do the course (assuming that academic criteria have been met). Should the decision be in the affirmative, an unobtrusive but immensely valuable role can be played by the medical team in assisting with any required treatment or medication. Just as importantly, they may also be able to carry out a form of medical counselling, helping the student to think through how realistic it is to pursue certain options, or to set particular social or academic targets.

Because of the increasing proportion of students with special needs, the University of Ulster has introduced a Protocol which identifies key personnel and stages in the assessment and meeting of needs both prior to arrival and after the commencement of the course. The team implementing the Protocol within Student Services consists of the Guidance and Welfare Officer and the nursing staff. (See Appendix III.)

Mental Health. Higher education of whatever mode may sometimes be perceived by people as a means of combating and overcoming mental health problems. These can range from reactive depressions after trauma or loss to psychotic episodes which have necessitated periods of hospitalization.

Once again an early contact with the medical team can confidentially advise the potential student as to the pace and expectations of academic life and the availability of specialist psychiatric services in the area should they be required. Reassurance is obviously automatically given that, if there is a need for continuation of stablizing drugs on prescription or psychotherapy, these issues will be sensitively and confidentially handled. There are many recorded instances where someone with a fine imaginative mind has been able to respond joyfully to the stimulating environment of a university and contribute to the collective good of the campus with the insightful help of the medical officer or nurse, when, a few months previously, extended hospitalization appeared to be the only other option.

Overseas Students. As discussed elsewhere, there are many difficulties which can loom large in the mind of overseas students going through the process of transition in a strange cultural environment. From the standpoint of their health, the close proximity of medical professionals is highly important in order that some basic but crucial questions can be addressed. A very fundamental area where explanation is needed is the nature of the National Health Service and the procedures involved in gaining temporary registration. It is easily forgotten that the scope of the NHS and its benefits is not a worldwide phenomenon! Other advice and information which will have long-term usefulness includes: nutritional issues and the implications of changes in diet; climatic differences and the relationship between sensible choice of clothing and wellbeing!

(b)Health Promotion

The brief time spent on campus can initiate and reinforce life-style practices and habits which will then generalize and influence the life of the student long after the academic course is completed, and for good or ill! Various individual and group projects can be initiated by the health team which stimulate the students to reflect on the balance in their social, personal and recreational life-styles, gaining optimal enjoyment yet ensuring sound physical and mental health and development.

Health Fairs. This is the ideal forum in which to engage students in informal group dialogue in a non-threatening and stimulating way. A large space is filled with a wide array of stalls chock-a-block with the wares of voluntary organizations and associations concerned with various aspects of healthy living. These could include: vegetarian societies, alcohol addiction centres, chest and heart associations, staff from the sport and recreation centre, the AIDS Lifeline team, the pregnancy advisory service. All manner of mysterious contraptions, tubes and dials invite the students to blow, suck, run, jump or lie down. Buzz group conversations can be heard in all corners on topics such as cholesterol levels, effects of smoking on a footballer's stamina, the symptomatology of bulimia and anorexia nervosa. Addresses are swopped and pamphlets are distributed. While the atmosphere is cheerful and light, the buzz has a certain substance to it. A well-advertised Health Fair around the middle of the autumn term can help the first year student to reflect a little on certain key decisions about life-style. It is accepting and non-judgemental; it does not prescribe; but it illuminates if the eye or the ear is willing.

Medical Counselling and Sexual Behaviour. It is an undeniable fact that the average eighteen year old student, male or female, has a modicum of accurate knowledge about sex and a whole paraphernalia of mythologies and distortions. At the same time the very stage of their physical and emotional development has to do with exploration in sexual relations. Choices are made constantly about new friendships, the degree of intimacy in those relationships and the responsibilities entailed in sharing private aspects of oneself with others. States of inadequate knowledge or emotional unreadiness manifest themselves in various ways on the campus. An unwanted pregnancy occurs because neither partner checked out precautionary measures properly; a level of intimacy develops too quickly for another couple and one of the partners seeks an escape route leaving the other in utter emotional disarray. When the natural and healthy drive to form intimate relationships becomes derailed and the personality has no precedent that will help cope with it, the repercussions can deeply affect everyday functioning and result in an underachieving student. Opportunities present themselves constantly to the health team in the course of apparently routine work to pick up on cues really relating to anxieties about sexual relations. Plain and direct information-giving may be all that is required, for instance about sexual hygiene or contraceptive aids. Or the help might be more on an emotional plane, when sensibilities have been deeply wounded by a partner. These matters are often inextricably connected with the students' struggle to grasp onto a coherent sense of personal identity; it is absolutely vital therefore that the health professional listens, accepts and works with the student on an adult to adult basis. Where a student has become pregnant, a highly delicate process of talking and thinking through the options and consequences of any decisions is obviously essential. Any temptation to step into the prescriptive parental role must be actively resisted as the young adult tries to work out and unravel her feelings, responsibilities and priorities. It could be that a range of alternatives will be considered from abortion, to departure from the institution, to adoption of the child , or staying on campus as a single parent with the child. Whatever the conclusion, it has to be reached at the student's own pace exercising self-determination.

Fear of Stigma. Much useful work can go on in the sphere of enhancing the self-confidence and self-image of students who fear that they may be perceived by their peers as deviant or different. Such students may present at the health service with conditions that are not obvious or visible to other people. It may be for instance an epileptic disorder, an asthmatic condition, a partial hearing loss. The student perhaps makes an appointment ostensibly presenting practical issues for discussion, but in fact wishing to confide anxieties of a psychological nature. Once again a willing listening ear and a friendly message that the student may return at any time just to talk without any particular reason may be enough to help the student keep matters in perspective. Or the staff may help the students by taking them through forms of behaviour rehearsal in which they anticipate stressful situations but by visualizing them in advance in the safety of the private session, they can then handle the real event more confidently. The issue in question might be as specific and practical as the asthmatic student rehearsing how to present a seminar paper before the rest of the student group and using relaxation techniques and breathing exercises to combat the anticipated rise in stress level.

On a more general level, the nurses and doctors should be able to develop informal friendly relationships with not just individuals but all manner of clubs and societies. The hockey club may call in as a group to get advice about their pending European tour. The swimming team want to sort out first aid arrangements for an inter-varsity gala which they are hosting. The aura has to be one of mutual trust and support – the collegiate spirit and the desire to help students gain optimum benefit from the whole social system of the educational establishment.

3. Counselling and Guidance

It is imperative that the practice of counselling is clearly differentiated from advice giving or exerting direct influence. A professional counsellor avoids transmitting values or stating preferences about solutions. Axiomatic to counselling practice is the belief that people should exercise self-determination over their own lives. Even if a crisis or dilemma has temporarily paralysed their coping capabilities, they can regain autonomy and find inner resources to resolve their difficulties. Awareness of their own ability to make decisions and act on their situations can instil confidence, and learning can generalize to future challenges making them better able to cope:

> ... the purpose of counselling is to facilitate wise choices of the sort on which
> the person's later development depends.   (L E Tyler 1969 p 13.)

In the course of resolution in the identified problem areas, the skills of the counsellor include listening, verbal and non-verbal reinforcement, interpreting and sometimes challenging. While theories of practice procedures vary, it is commonly accepted that much of the effectiveness of counselling is linked to the establishing of a trusting rapport between the counsellor and the person concerned. This rapport is undoubtedly closely associated with the counsellor's ability to convey attitudes that are accepting, non-judgemental and respecting of confidentiality.

There are various instances, related to the time phases of students' educational progress, when the role of the counsellor can be immensely beneficial to the student' personal development.

The Initial Decision. At the point when a person is weighing up the possibility of entering higher education, before a formal application is even lodged, access to a counsellor who has no economic vested interest in the outcome of the decision can have a useful unlocking effect on that person's motivation. It might be the school-leaver talking to the school counsellor or the mature person approaching the educational guidance service attached to the local technical college or the college's own counsellor. So many implications of the change of role can be effectively addressed in advance. Perhaps an aptitude questionnaire can be administered and the results used as an aid to discussion. With the school-leaver, thinking through of choices that might mean living away from home for the first time might be rehearsed. The mature adult might be concerned about potential drop in income and effects on relationships and responsibilities within the family. Whatever the areas which are explored in the biographical context of the people concerned, the opportunity to think through the possible consequences of decisions will probably have long-term benefits. In contrast there have been too many casualties within the higher education system who have invested greatly in time and energy and made far-reaching personal sacrifices only to discover that the particular course chosen or the general ethos of the institutions were not in tune with their needs.

The Induction Process. Sensitive work by counsellors alongside the academic departments can make a positive impact on adaptation to academic life. In a typical session between counsellors and first year students, certain key principles would operate: there would be a warm and informal message of welcome; information overload would be avoided at all costs; sessions would be structured in small groups so that students could be introduced to each other without threat or embarrassment. Key messages which would hopefully be received by the students would be that they have lots of common ground with people who a few hours before were total strangers: and that "those people from Student Services are available to us as individuals if we ever need them".

Identity Crisis. A few days or weeks into the start of the first term, some students have serious doubts about the wisdom of their decision to come. It may be related ostensibly to the nature of the course, the general environment away from home, the continuation of unresolved demands or problems which the students left behind at home:

> Peer groups and friends often exert a powerful influence on the ways that university students think and behave. The family system continues to be extremely important, even though students may be somewhat more removed from their families than in earlier stages of life. They are learning to assume roles in their families that are more independent than ones they have filled in the past. They may be challenged to examine old values and in the process

may encounter more conflict with parents.

One of the liabilities of the human power to think is that our interpersonal systems remain operative on a cognitive level long after they have ceased to exist in the world. In our heads we may still hear the voice of a mother who is no longer living. We can also maintain the mental model of a parent's behaviour after the behaviour itself has undergone change. Thus family systems are not just of historical significance even if they no longer exist in the outside world. They are a part of our present worlds – the ones we maintain in our minds. The roles we learned to play in our families are often related to more generalized concepts of how we should live our lives with other people.   (J C Barrow 1986 p 128.)

It is helpful in such instances if the studies adviser can encourage the student to seek out the counsellor assuming the student has not already done so. A climate in which the student can air any anxiety and consider any option without fear of offending anyone or setting up conflicts of roles is usually preferable. Eventually the student may decide to remain, or to transfer onto another programme of studies (an option which every institution should permit up to the end of the first month). Alternatively it could be better to leave because the longer term personal development of the student will be more satisfactorily served in some other educational institution or career field.

Another situation in which identity crises can arise is when the student's name does not appear on the Examination Officer's board, and the reality of failure has to be faced. Once again good liaison between the academic department, Student Services and Academic Registry is essential to ensure that the student received support if desired. In this context, as in all others, the counsellor will once again help the student examine and think through options but will avoid direct influence and prescription. The central tenet in this case would also be that, by confronting the failure and dealing with it, the student can learn from it and it becomes another source of constructive personal development.

Individual Casework and Groupwork. Most of the counsellor's work takes place on a one-to-one basis with students. The focus of the work is wide-ranging – estranged relationships in the family, reactive depression after bereavement, marital disharmony, learning difficulties, drug or alcohol abuse, problems in self-assertion, role changes or conflicts. While much of the work is reactive in the sense that the student identifies an existent problem, there are many opportunities for proactive initiatives. Examples include: the convening of voluntary study skills groups in which students' active participation is encouraged. Topics such as attitudes to learning are discussed and how these are affected by earlier life experiences. Often there is a valuable collaborative approach when academic staff from a particular Faculty might act as co-leaders to provide a 'specialist' input while the counsellor addresses more 'generic' principles. Other groups which are again convened on a voluntary basis when interest is expressed include mature students groups, assertiveness training and relaxation sessions.

Ensuring Natural Justice. With the students' consent, counsellors can also submit reports to examination boards if special circumstances need to be drawn to their attention that might have affected academic performance. This helps to ensure that fast and equitable decisions are made.

Guidance and Assessment. As student numbers increase, there is a need for specialist practitioners in the counselling and guidance team. For instance, with student maintenance grants frozen, there is growing evidence of student problems linked to acute financial strain. As a consequence, students benefit from updated information about grant-awarding organizations, advice about DHSS benefit entitlements, eligibility for university endowment or Access Funds.

A welcome feature of widened access is the significant proportion of student entrants with special needs arising from disability, specific learning difficulties or socio-economic backgrounds. However, it is encumbent on universities to develop comprehensive protocols which ensure that special needs are assessed and relevant responses are determined before students commence their studies. To facilitate these services, some counselling and guidance teams now employ educational or clinical psychologists.

Inter-Professional Co-operation. Close professional co-operation is obviously required between all the staff dealing with students' personal affairs. For instance a student interest group might be formed as a result of a Health Fair, and expresses the wish to explore personal life styles. The health team carried out a battery of tests and measurements on areas such as cholesterol level and blood pressure levels and a baseline profile is built up on each participating student. The counsellor interview the students to discuss any personal or social implications arising from the findings and whether any amendments to life patterns is desirable. The Sport Centre staff discuss various routes to greater fitness from which the students can choose elements that they think will be compatible with their preferred modes of living. There are both short term and long term benefits which the students accrue. In the current life situation, better physical and mental fitness permeates general outlook and self-confidence, and academic performance is enhanced. In the long term, habits have been instilled which will prolong good health and general coping capacity.

4. The Careers Advisory Service

It has been emphasized throughout this work that universities must not become training schools preparing students in specific skills and slotting them into pre-determined pigeon-holes in the world of commerce, industry and public service. In the same vein, careers advisory officers must not become mere unquestioning mediators between the academic institutions and the world of work outside. Attempts to move towards a privatized placement agency model of careers service are ill-advised. Having said that, the careers advisers provide a key service from which students can gain depths of insight about their own aptitudes and future roles.

There are several basic aims in a comprehensive careers advisory service. Firstly it aims to help students to understand the process of career choice and to develop their capabilities to determine and execute immediate and later career decisions. Reciprocally the service should aim to help the University to understand and adapt to the changing employment market for graduates. Marketing is an essential ingredient too, as the service vaunts the merits of graduates to employers. Because of the rapidly changing needs, the service should continually seek to maintain and improve the standard of professional provision. Other roles include the provision of support for related areas of activity such as schools liaison, placements and the Enterprise in Higher Education initiative.

It is useful to consider the purposes of the careers advisory service in terms of five phases. In practice, students may make use of the service in the following ways:

a) **Prior to arrival** – Careers education programmes are made available to help students to consider the career implications of course choices.

b) **During first year** – Students may be helped to choose subject options for subsequent years; guidance may be given to those who wish to change courses or discontinue; others may receive information about work experience or part-time vacation employment.

c) **During second year** – Students may be encouraged to explore opportunities available and how they relate to their own hopes, values, interests and abilities.

d) **During final year** – At this point the practicalities are highlighted of: how to get information on vacancies; how to focus on relevant employers; how to select suitable post-graduate courses.

e) **After graduation** – Graduates may continue to use the service if and when they are considering a change in career.

Effective guidance must be backed up by an up-to-date and comprehensive information facility, emphasizing the importance of regular close links with employers and effective liaison with the Association of Graduate Careers Advisory Services (AGCAS) and the Association of Graduate Recruiters (AGR). Increasingly computer-aided guidance systems are becoming available such as 'Prospect', a generic program which assists with career planning irrespective of the subjects studied. AGCAS provides a crucial support network through the organisation of professional training, exchange of information, and the establishment of working parties to research areas of general interest, such as the needs of older graduates. This means that issues which no one service could deal with individually are effectively addressed.

As with the other support services, the careers advisory service should aim to contribute to the personal development of students throughout their university careers. Essentially the service is a personalised confidential one and therefore has to maintain an identity independent of the academic departments. However, it is important that the careers advisers, in as far as ethical considerations permit, do work with academic staff and try to reach agreement on the best type of careers input for their students. This is usually only possible in a groupwork context as individual discussions with careers advisers are of necessity confidential.

Manifestly this is a highly skilled professional area ranging from the provision of a receptive and welcoming environment to the counselling skills required in a personal interview. Far from being the descriptive provision of laundry lists of job vacancies, the good careers advisory service help students to achieve a clarity of vision and maximise their personal potential.

> Careers guidance is concerned with complex and controversial matters. It operates in the interface between individual choices and societal choices, individual needs and societal needs. From the individual's point-of-view, paid employment – which traditionally has been the central preoccupation of careers guidance – is a powerful determinant not only of income but also of social status and family life, as well as determining how a major part of one's waking hours will be spent. From society's point-of-view, the effectiveness with which manpower is deployed is an important determinant of its economic health. Choosing an occupation can indeed be seen as a key contractual transaction between the individual and society, through which individuals offer some of their time and energies to pursue societal purposes, in return for money and other rewards which will sustain their private lives.

> (A G Watts, B Law & B Fawcett 1981 p 374.)

5. Nursery Playgroup Provision

Historically in universities, assistance has only been given to child-minding projects in the form of free accommodation. Thus such enterprises have had to be entirely self-financing, apart from subsidized rent and rates. In practice this has meant that a wide range of facilities exist throughout the universities with variable standards, and sometimes highly questionable conditions of service for the caring staff. It is often difficult to prevent the fees from becoming totally prohibitive because of the self-financing constraints. Students' Unions either help to run facilities or contribute indirectly by underwriting part or all of the student parents' fees. The rudimentary nature of many nursery playgroups on campus reflects the low priority accorded to them. In these modern times, it has long since been accepted that mature women have a right to enter higher education if they have the interest and potential. It is also recognized by most observers that women with families find it difficult to focus without anxiety on academic study unless satisfactory arrangements have been made for the care of their children. If there is no stability in the arrangements the woman can become racked with guilt even if rationally she has tried to step outside stereotypic assumptions about the primary caring role of the mother-figure. It makes a nonsense of foundation courses geared towards raising the awareness of mature women if academic institutions do not provide child-minding facilities which have: high child care standards; qualified staff; sufficient per capita places to meet projected needs; and which charge fees which are not prohibitive.

Because of the importance of good standards and efficient administration, such facilities should be integrated within the official Student Services and not left to the voluntary efforts of parents or charitable groups. They must be viewed as fundamental prerequisites to enable many parents to make the decision to enter higher education in the first instance and then do themselves full justice in their academic pursuits.

Other elements of academic life and organisation conducive to Personal Development.

The Role of the Students' Union

Over the last few years, anxieties bordering on moral panic have been evident both at the level of the educational authorities and at governmental level about the functions and motivation of the National Union of Students. In particular allegations about political bias and 'closed shop' practices have led to a House of Commons investigation.

It is to be hoped that properly funded students' unions will continue to receive the full support of the universities . When the cross-section of activities under their umbrella is analysed, they clearly provide much stimulus to students for constructive action and personal growth. The administration of the wide range of clubs and societies by student' union officers ensures that sport, drama, music, conservation, debating societies, chess clubs, and a host of other activities have the chance to thrive on campus. Links with the wider community are manifold through activities such as charitable fund-raising, welfare rights projects, volunteer work with the elderly and the disabled. Through membership of committees, students can gain .invaluable representative experience and learn the arts of negotiation, compromise and the handling of conflict. The sabbatical officers also provide peer group welfare and housing advice services for students and take on advocacy roles from time to time in ways that would not be appropriate for the college's officers.

Of immense significance, the National Union of Students has recently published a Students' Charter which seeks to enunciate fundamental principles of higher education and the basic rights of students. Cogent arguments are made about flexible access and participation, but it is also notable that emphasis is placed on the responsibility of students for their own learning and the importance of partnership within educational institutions. Not only is this an invaluable contribution to the wider debate, it has also shown the way to the British Government which, at the time of writing, has still not produced its own Higher Education Charter.

The Chaplaincy

Spirituality and reflection on non-materialist concerns should play an intrinsic part in the personal development of university students. For some it will take the form of a 'secular' spirituality, located in the social interaction between people and not determined by any form of intangible Deity – the discovery of a faith in fellow human beings. On the other hand, many students have a need for spiritual succour and guidance from the more traditional sources of the chaplains. It is essential, therefore, that the voluntary option to seek such friendship and support should always be available and accessible on campus.

Academic Registry as the first point of contact

So often the first communication received by the students is not from the academic departments but from the officials of the Academic Registry of the Faculty Administrative Officers. This is a particularly susceptible and malleable time for students when good anticipatory work can be carried out in making the transition process easier and more manageable. Whether it be through written communications and instructions or group induction meetings at the start of term, certain key

principles are fundamentally important:
> avoidance of information overload;
> clear communication of accurate essential information about contact persons;
> early timetable commitments;
> administrative procedures for fee-paying and so on.

Most crucially important is the tone in which this information is delivered. The antennae of the new students pick up very quickly the underlying messages behind the material and the conclusion is reach – is this a friend or a foe! Much useful work can also be carried out by Academic Registry with overseas students when early postal communications of concise instructions makes the difference between calmness and chaos. In some institutions, Academic Registry and Student Services combine very effectively to run special induction programmes for the new overseas students prior to the beginning of the teaching term.

At the University of Ulster, this co-operation had led to the formation of International Committees which include representatives from the local communities, international students and interested university staff. These Committees contribute to the induction programmes and generally help to foster cross-cultural integration. The terms of reference of these Committees are given in Appendix IV.

The Sport and Recreation Department

Once again, with regard to a holistic approach to personal development, the practices adopted by the Sports Centre can have a profound influence on the wellbeing of the students. Apart from the provision of the outdoor and indoor sports facilities, imaginative initiatives have been developed in recent years in the area of prevention. These include: sports injuries consultative services with whom individuals or clubs can consult to ensure that the body can operate at peak performance and not break down through inadequate care or preparation; compilation of fitness profiles tailored to suit the individual disposition and physique of the student.

The Sports Centre activities, the 'Fun Runs', the reception of visiting teams from other institutions or the wider community all contribute greatly in making the campus a colourful and fertile environment for maturation and growth.

The Library Service

Often stereotyped as pedestrian and unexciting, the library service is in fact at the very heart of academic life, and can strongly influence the development of the students. It is also an arena surrounding which there can be a great aura of mystification, off-putting even to the most able student.

Catalogues, indexes, microfiche machines, visual display units, microcomputers, all present a formidable array of cul-de-sacs, one-way streets and roundabouts which the new student has to learn to negotiate in the quest for knowledge. Fortunately most library systems are now well geared to the needs of the students at group and individual levels. An introduction to the use of the library during the academic course induction programmes is also useful if carried out concisely or even in a series of small group meetings. Readers' advisers can subsequently be of great support to the individual students who need to pursue specialized or technical information and are still in the process of working out sources of information. Professional librarian skills are highlighted in this context in the sense that the nervous, under-confident or confused student needs an attentive and clearly interested listener and then a helpful explanation and clues to further actions and directions that can be taken. The nature and quality of these early contacts has a profound influence on how the students adapt to the world of scholarship. Libraries should always be enticing places in which to indulge one's intellectual curiosity, and never places where barriers are erected and alienation and avoidance are reinforced in the students. Their importance is also continuous throughout the students' courses although the emphasis on the usage will change depending on the time phase. By the time the undergraduates commence the final year dissertation, demonstration of their ability to take responsibility for their own pursuit of knowledge and scholarly research will be significantly correlated with the extent to which they have been encouraged to develop sound habits and disciplines in library use.

With the rapid advances in information technology, there are real opportunities to promote independent learning within the library system. In addition to quick access to sources, technology may soon offer the possibility of multiple electronic scanning of textbook material, which could provide radical solutions to the challenges of mass higher education and the potential expense of book purchases.

In the realm of special needs there is a strong argument for learning resource centres within libraries, including talk-back, print enlargement and electronic braille embossing facilities.

The Integrated Model and Personal Transferable Skills
By the provision of a coherent and integrated network of academic and support services, universities can maximize the opportunities for their students to develop personal transferable skills and attitude in the following key areas:

> interpersonal skills of communication;
> decision-making skills and strategies;
> capacity for teamwork;
> leadership qualities;

flexibility in attitude;

initiative and positive motivation;

ability to identify sources of information and conduct research.

In recent years the 'Enterprise in Higher Education' units established by universities have successfully overcome early scepticism about their role, and are now encouraging and funding a range of projects which are aimed at developing these transferable skills.

Not only do these enhanced qualities lead to a mature and roundly developed graduate personality, they also represent the ingredients that are avariciously sought by employers in all professions and fields of work. Whether it be the practice of law, the applied sciences and technology, business and commerce, or the Arts, it is recognized more and more by employers that if they are to thrive, they need to recruit people with creative imagination and initiative in their keys posts. In the field of education, it is vital to the wellbeing of future generations that institutions of higher education produce skilled and enthusiastic teachers who can inspire and stimulate.

In a truly democratic society, all citizens should be able to participate and contribute according to their abilities and receive in return social justice and the means to pursue a reasonable quality of life. Universities should be in the business of finely honing the talents of their students and enhancing their social awareness so that they can emerge as vital (if not always strictly conventional!) contributors to this process, both nationally and internationally.

Some Illustrative Case Studies

(The names are fictitious but the circumstances are factual)

In each of the following case studies, it is clearly identified that social and emotional factors can often have a significant influence on the academic progress of all students; and that close liaison between academic departments and support services is always vitally important if such students are to be helped to realize their full potential.

1. John's family live in Zambia. He himself was sent to England to further his education at the age of fourteen. Prior to entering university he spent four years in two different boarding schools. During vacations, he stayed with an elderly aunt in the Midlands who was a strict disciplinarian. As a young child he was humiliated regularly by a violently aggressive father who regarded him as a failure, not fit to be the eldest son of the family. Probably directly related to this, John is distinctively lacking in self-esteem although he is intelligent. He also finds it difficult to form new personal relationships with females who tend to find his

attention-seeking hyperactive behaviour too childlike and immature. Being black, he has also been subjected to racist abuse, both verbal and physical. John has chosen to undertake a degree course in environmental science.

His first year at university has been very unsettled. He has had accommodation problems, and has been scapegoated by other members of the student group, being treated as a figure of ridicule. His academic work has been patchy, and highly descriptive and conservative. However one key change in his life-style has a very significant ripple effect into other areas of his life. A supportive accommodation officer helps him to find a new bed-sitter close to the campus. She knows the resident landlady personally as someone who does not inappropriately interfere in students' lives but does take a personal interest in their welfare. She develops an immediate liking for John which gradually becomes tantamount to a mother-substitute relationship. Far from feeling smothered by this, John begins to thrive in the affectionate concern. He shares the house with four other students, who, although attending different courses form a fairly cohesive group and incorporate John in their social activities. One of them encourages John to join him in the university basket ball club and his self-esteem soars when he discovers he has hitherto untapped abilities in this sport. He becomes visibly less insecure in his behaviour and some of his irritating attention-seeking behaviour starts to recede. He is now becoming more receptive to new ideas, and more willing to risk himself in his academic work.

2. Edgar is twenty two years old. He left school at sixteen and has travelled around Britain and Europe doing various part-time jobs. His parents are working class manual workers by background and there is no history of attendance at university in the family. They have long since regarded Edgar as a misfit who did not fulfil his duty to them by getting a proper full-time job and paying money into the household. They are now emotionally estranged from him and he does not feel welcome in their home. He has accepted a place at the university on a degree course in English Literature.

The first few days of the course turn out to be riddled with crisis. Because of the grant regulations, he does not qualify for independent student status – he has not accrued sufficient income over the previous three years. Consequently his parents are required to submit declarations of their income but they have refused to do so. A concerned studies adviser contacts the counsellor and arranges an appointment stating that Edgar has said he is about to leave the university. The fact that he has no financial means has had a deep emotional as well as practical effect on Edgar. He reveals to the counsellor that feelings of anger and confusion have welled up in him and he feels like a powerless child again. As a result of this crisis, his academic career may literally come to a sudden halt. However some quiet, sensitive work on the counsellor's part helps to resolve the situation. A small interest-free loan is arranged from university funds to bring some temporary relief. With the student's consent, the relevant scholarships officer in the local education authority is contacted and sympathetically agrees to a partial advance on the grant while reasserting that he has to act within the grant regulations and still has to carry out an assessment of the parental income.

Edgar has continued his studies and is satisfied that he made the right decision in coming to university. He is still working on the deeper personal issue of rejection by his parents. With the help of the counsellor, he has been able to visit the parental home and open up communication again for the first time in a number of years.

3. Margaret is thirty two years old and has two children under five years of age. At the age of eighteen, she made a decision to live with her boyfriend rather than continue with her education. Subsequently they married and she had the youngsters in rapid succession. Marital relations broke down in dire and hurtful circumstances, and Margaret left with the children. She has now set up as a single parent in a flat in distinctly reduced material and financial circumstances.

Having commenced her degree course in Philosophy, her performance was initially very promising and motivation high. However attendance begins to be patchy coursework deadlines are missed and her physical appearance is causing the senior course tutor concern. She is encouraged to make an appointment with the medical officer. It transpires that she is under great personal pressure in that her husband is pressing for the custody of the two children on the grounds that she is not a fit person. He is focusing on the fact that she leaves them with an assortment of friends or casual contacts while she attends the university. On her reduced income, this has been literally her only alternative, although she states that she is very concerned about their welfare. Her constant worry, like some grotesque self-fulfilling prophesy, is detrimentally affecting her coping ability and giving her the appearance of an 'unfit person'. Medication is prescribed by the medical officer who also contacts the university nursery playgroup supervisor with her consent and arranges an appointment. She is informed that fees for the child care are subsidized according to needs by the Students' Union, and she is impressed by the standards of care demonstrated by the staff.

Margaret is now back in regular attendance on her course. She has established a good rapport with her studies adviser and has joined a mature students group. However she is still thinking through the different demands on her, some highly conflicting. Not least she reflects on the balance between her right to pursue her own personal development and her 'duties and responsibilities' as a parent.

4. Mary is eighteen years old and is highly independent in spirit. Her coursework essays on the History degree have been of a very creditable standard showing critical ability and breadth of reading. However the examinations have been surprisingly disappointing to the internal examiners, with one resit being required at the end of the summer vacation.

There is an evident gulf between proven potential and performance – she is grossly under-achieving. One comment made by an alert invigilator is passed on to the studies adviser by Academic Registry. In the course of one examination, Mary was observed squinting very intensely at the paper which she held just a few inches away from her glasses. In a follow-up interview with Mary, Student Services has established that she is in fact registered as partially sighted! However she decided not to bring this fact to the attention of the academic department because she was anxious not to be regarded as 'different' from fellow students. She had arrived at the university with no close friends, and believed that she would be more acceptable if she acted as 'normally' as possible.

After an assessment of the extent of her disability, Mary was given various options for special examination arrangements. She has decided to continue in the same examination hall as her peer group, but will be given papers with specially enlarged print and will be allowed an additional half hour to complete the paper. The medical officer has also arranged to have her supplied with a special ocular aid.

5. Mr 'X' is a student from a Middle Eastern country. While he was completing 'A' Levels at a technical college in Britain, his country became involved in a war. His parents, who still reside in the home country, urged him to continue his studies at university and pledged him financial support. During his first year studies, he received word from home that his government was no longer prepared to authorize foreign currency transactions from his parents. There was also a direct implication in correspondence that he was expected to return home immediately and join the armed forces. He does not support the political regime in his country and did not wish to return to fight in the war. With his parents' consent, he is continuing his studies but has no form of income to sustain him. In the meantime one of his brothers has been killed in action and he has not been able to attend his funeral. A highly intelligent student, his thoughts are distressingly preoccupied with unresolved grief about his brother, and concern that he may not be able to complete his degree. The careers officer has been giving him support as he tries to think through the options for his future career. He also meets with staff from Academic Registry and Student Services from time to time as he is contemplating seeking 'exceptional leave to remain' from the Home Office which would give him the entitlements of a home-based student but could affect his government's attitudes to his national

identity. In the background, the university has a useful liaison with the United Kingdom Council for Overseas Students Affairs and is able to update the student about current official procedures and policies.

6. Student 'B' is a postgraduate research student from the Far East. She achieved a primary degree of an excellent standard in her home country but is finding the transition into a British university difficult. She perceives the approach to education as culturally different from her experience and this is setting up strain between her and her supervisor. One of the sources of tension is that the supervisor identifies her faltering command of the English language as the major cause of lack of progress. Miss 'B' disputes this and maintains that she has not tuned into the different approaches used. She confides to a counsellor that her confidence is rapidly being undermined but she cannot present herself to her supervisor and the Faculty as she pictures herself, a widely read and competent person. The counsellor has also been approached by one of the representatives of the overseas students committee expressing concern about Miss 'B''s plight. As an attempt to address the difficulties, Miss 'B', the counsellor and the research supervisor have agreed to hold a tripartite meeting.

7. Alan arrived at the university through the UCCA clearing house system just after teaching term had started. Fortunately he was able to move into the Student Residences because of a cancellation. After a few days the behaviour of this student, who is in his late twenties, begins to cause concern among fellow students. He wanders around at night-time, takes small items of food from other students' lockers, and generally look very withdrawn and bizarre. A senior residential student approaches the Warden of Halls and asks if he could investigate. 'Dropping in' for a coffee with the student in his room, the Warden discovers that Alan has spent the last two years in a psychiatric hospital. He studied for his 'A' Levels at evening classes and applied for a place on the Computer Studies course as a 'second chance' attempt to carve out a career for himself. Because of the lateness of the confirmation of the offer of a place, Alan travelled to the university in a rush and totally overlooked the question of medication. As a result he has been experiencing florid and distressing symptoms and has been so disorientated in the new environment that he did not know where he could go for assistance. The Warden contacts the medical officer with the student's consent, who arranges continuation of medication having contacted the hospital. In addition, the senior residential student and the Warden give feedback to the students who had been expressing concern. The students, hearing some of the background from the Warden and Alan himself, show the beginnings of a positive acceptance of him and peer group support.

8. Angela approaches the careers officer in some distress. She has been bottling up feelings of great rejection for several months since she applied, at the end of first year, for a delayed choice place on her preferred degree option and was turned down by the selection panel. Immensely able but emotionally vulnerable, she felt that her total personality had been dismissed by this decision. In addition, she is under the erroneous impression that her last hope of gaining this particular professional qualification has disappeared. It is clear that the university system has failed her because of the peremptory selection procedure, and the inadequacy of the information provided about alternative routes. The careers advisory officer is able to clarify that there is an alternative postgraduate route and that the primary degree she is studying will be acceptable and cognate. To strengthen her case for a postgraduate place, the careers advisory officer also puts Angela in touch with employers in order to gain some relevant practical experience during the summer vacation. A potentially debilitating depression lifts for the student. However, to minimize the chances of a recurrence with other students, the careers advisory officer has a quiet word with the relevant academic head of department about first year delayed choice selection procedures.

9. Jim is twenty three and has congenital spina bifida. He is a wheelchair user but can also walk with callipers for short distances. His secondary education has been badly disrupted because of various periods of hospitalization during which he underwent many operations. However, through additional evening class study at a local technical college, he has managed to obtain eight 'O' Levels.

After discussion with a senior course tutor from the Faculty of Science, he decides to apply for a special Foundation Course in Science, a one year full-time course geared to prepare students for later undergraduate study. He is accepted onto the course, and the senior course tutor invites him to meet representatives from Student Services and the academic department for an 'individualized assessment'. Although he is very independent in nature (possibly excessively so), he agrees that this would be desirable. The nurse for the campus discusses his medical history and likely follow-up contacts with the hospital; the accommodation officer shows him a specially adapted ground floor flat in the Student Residences and takes some notes on other special needs that he has where minor works modification would help – for instance, an additional fixed shelf for his micro computer; the academic tutor, after feedback about mobility, discusses with him plans for the arrangement of tutorials and seminars in accessible areas. Peter is also given a booklet outlining all the access routes (eg to library, Students' Union, etc), location of adapted toilets, names of designated people in Academic Registry, Library, Student Services, and all the key departments with whom he can make contact at any time.

10. Rosemary is from a family of six children, of whom she is the eldest. The family live in a rural part of Ireland where the attitude about male and female roles are very traditional and inflexible. Her two brothers are in their teens and help out in their free time on the farm. Having married late, her father and mother are relatively elderly and becoming somewhat frail.

Having surpassed all expectations with excellent results in her Leaving Certificate (equivalent to 'A' Levels but broader) she has opted for a university education. After six months, she breaks down in her studies adviser's room and intimate that she is under great pressure from her parents to give up the course in languages and return to help with the family affairs. It has reached the point where communication has broken down, and the father is no longer sending money. She has stopped going home for occasional week-ends because the atmosphere is so emotionally fraught. At the same time she does not receive any state grant and is virtually penniless. Following an interview with the Student Services welfare assistant an application is lodged successfully with the University Scholarships Committee for a special award from an Endowment Fund. This will only cover short-term expenses but the Students' Union has put her in touch with a local firm for part-time employment.

Rosemary is still feeling very isolated and has chosen to visit the University Chaplain regularly for spiritual guidance.

Chapter Six

Assurance of Quality

Universities are not tertiary training schools. Attempts to impel them in this direction would deprive the country of a vital creative resource. In reality, historically-bound political dogmatists and private entrepreneurs do not have a sufficient breadth of vision to define the role of higher education – they are propelled by current ideological prescriptions and short-term materialistic gains. For an increasingly broad cross-section of the population, third level institutions should in contrast offer a fertile environment for thought, an intellectual culture where curiosity can be assuaged, where the exasperating limits and uncertainties of knowledge can be recognized with humility and tolerance. They should be forums in which all manner of ideas, however objectionable, are given a hearing but are also held up to public analysis and criticism:

> But even in authoritarian regimes, someone is needed to point out the fallibility of rulers and to play the part of the child who sees and says that the Emperor has no clothes. (J Barnes and N Barr 1088 p 1.)

Seven hundred and eighty years on from the inception of the very first British university, the social context and the nature and needs of the students have changed radically. There must be a willingness on the part of the modern universities to accept and enact their responsibilities in relation to wider society. Their students should be encouraged to learn from a dialectical engagement with the surrounding world, not be enshrined in a smug, self-sufficient cocoon. The fruits of their scholarship and research should be made available to the wider community, not in a directive sense, but in order to enable the citizenry and their political representatives to make informed choices. In these ways, they would be fulfilling a profoundly important public service essential to the growth and prosperity of democratic society. As this would necessitate predominantly public funding, both for the functioning of academic institutions and the maintenance of their students, clear procedures for accountability must exist to ensure that the taxpayers are receiving full value for money. Among the ways of demonstrating this accountability, full community representation on the governing bodies and publicly available feedback on the activities of the institutions are but two imperatives.

With regard to the individual student, it has been maintained throughout this book that the university, possibly more so than many environments, can promote the personal development of its students in the broadest sense. Whatever the age group of the students, or the mode of study which they have undertaken, the climate established on campus should offer stimulation intellectually, socially, emotionally and culturally. The transformations which can take place as a result are not in the form of mystical and detached elitism – lessons in how to regard oneself as superior or different. Rather insights and awareness which result should induce a humble congeniality and tolerance in the students, and ambitions to help service their community. Their heightened powers of critical analysis and qualities of questioning and scepticism should ensure that, whatever their actual working roles are in their careers, their society benefits from their continually challenging vitality. This is in total contrast to the utilitarian assumption that people should be trained to fit into part of a production line and should obediently remember their places at all times. In essence the entire argument in this book has been a celebration of a horticultural growth model of personal development and a refutation of the stultifying and constraining effects of modern utilitarianism. It is also arguable that these underlying principles of personal development should be applied positively to all people in whatever sector of society, and not just students in higher education.

What follows is a summary of the major recommendations which have emanated from the discussion in order to promote an effective climate for personal development. These recommendations range from the 'political' to the 'personal', making demands on the 'social' systems as much as the individuals.

Politics and Policy

Higher education should be funded predominantly from the public purse. The political vision informing future policy should be that there is a long-term investment for society in ensuring that universities not only equip their graduates with skills and knowledge, but with a questioning openness and a preparedness to explore new boundaries. In this respect, mandatory maintenance grants must be made available to all students, index-linked and not dependent on parental assessment. Top-up loans should be abolished in favour of a salary-related graduate tax, which would be acceptable to the vast majority of students.

Academic institutions should identify closely with local geographical regions, encouraging full community involvement in their activities, including their policy-making bodies. Far from reinforcing provincial incestuousness, such collaboration should be in the spirit of demystifying higher education, and enhancing the awareness of the general public about the accessibility of universities.

While being publicly accountable for their activities and expenditure, however, universities must retain the right of freedom of expression and the pursuit of learning and research for their own sake. Particularly at this historical point, when economic stringency coupled with increased student numbers demands a scrupulous and businesslike approach to ensure survival, it is necessary to stand firm by first principles! Otherwise the dangerous scenario could develop whereby course and research selectivity to guarantee revenue might lead to an actual repression of the pursuit of knowledge. Indeed institutions of higher education must not be compelled to follow the diktats of any one political party or ideology. As indicated by the rapidly changing social and political climate in Central and Eastern Europe, it is extremely important that universities have the self-confidence to work alongside governments but never be dominated by them. In all respects, therefore, the Charter or Mission Statement should be regarded as sacrosanct, a symbol of strength.

Institutional Procedures within Universities
On a practical level, universities should literally be open to the public on a flexible basis both in terms of hours of opening and modes of courses. More and more establishments are introducing a modular approach to course delivery, wherein a student may complete a self-sufficient and assessed period of study within a semester. This opens up greater flexibility in terms of either extending the length of a degree or 'fast-tracking' the course in a shorter period. It is now also possible, under 'credit accumulation and transfer', to complete modules at different universities. Complementary to these structural developments, universities should pursue the creation of 'out-centres' and college houses in various parts of the region, thus increasing access and identification with the whole community.

A holistic approach to the planning of the academic year is essential. Joint instructions and information bulletins for new students should be regularly reviewed to ensure that they remain attuned to the modern needs of the students. It is so easy to make misplaced assumptions about the relevance of material which is a few years old. With the rapid developments in the arena of information technology, there are now great opportunities to ensure that information is fresh, updated, well-reasoned, and available at the push of a terminal keyboard. Other financial priorities should be supported as an investment in the enrichment of collegiate life. These should include: high quality nursery provision; student residences alongside an appropriate network of off-campus accommodation. With regard to the building of additional student residences, the University Funding Council should rescind the bar on the use of capital grant which has applied since the 1970s, and provide tangible and substantial assistance to those British universities which have urgent need of more residential bed-places. Policies concerning the intake of overseas students must be based on the cross-cultural and academic benefits to be derived, and the honest confidence that facilities exist to honour contracts to the students' satisfaction; not merely or predominantly for reasons of gaining additional revenue (Caul 1991).

Faculty Imperatives

There will always be a necessity for the role of 'studies adviser' in Faculty departments; someone who teaches on the student's course and is available to offer advice and guidance if any obstacles appear in the way of academic progress. Such roles should be clearly defined and given some formal recognition in the form of contract hours allowance. As Faculties increase in size, there is also an argument in favour of co-ordinating personnel in Faculties, be they senior course tutors, directors or specifically appointed, part of whose role is to ensure that the department is aware of appropriate sources of help; to stimulate good practice among studies advisers; to organize staff development; and initiate student groupwork activities which promote independent learning.

Entry into the novel environment of a campus can be a daunting experience both for school-leavers and mature students. To assist with this vital phase of orientation, each course should offer an initial induction programme during which students can meet informally with fellow students and tutors; individual meetings between students and studies advisers should also be arranged at an early stage and assurance given as appropriate in relation to 'settling in' issues. Because of the flexible entry points associated with modular courses, planned induction programmes should be organized at the beginning of each semester.

Integrated Learner Support Services

Complementing the teaching and studies advice within Faculties, it is important to have a coherent and integrated range of key support services for the learner. Preferably, in management terms, these services should be encompassed within one department with its own devolved budget and overall ethos. There is a compelling case that counselling and guidance, health, accommodation and careers advice should be encompassed within this framework. All are confidential, individualised services central to the objective of maximizing the personal development of learners. The ethos of these services should emphasize physical and attitudinal accessibility, and non-stigmatising universality.

The Students' Union

It is also essential to the wellbeing of students that they have access to a Students'

Union, an autonomous service which provides both peer support and, if appropriate, advocacy. The Students' Union has a vital role in developing social responsibility and awareness in students and should remain as a key service on campus. It is probably desirable that future students be given the voluntary choice of joining the Students' Union, if this removes the negative label of 'a closed shop'. In addition, since the term 'Union' is increasingly being viewed as a misnomer, this service would not lose its impact if it changed its title to 'Students' Representative Council' or some such alternative.

Educational Support Services

With the increasing emphasis on independent learning and information technology, there is a strong argument for greater collaboration, perhaps even within the same organizational sub-structure, between academic registry, the library and computer and audio-visual services. Indeed those institutions which aspire to relatively large increases in student numbers could combine such administrative linking with the imaginative development of self-pacing 'learning resource centres', strategically placed at various points on the campus.

Social and Recreational Services

Intrinsic to the health and development of students are the facilities offered by the sport and recreation services. Far from being isolated adjuncts, these services should be integrated carefully into the corporate plan of the university and given adequate resources. Similarly, the option of spiritual support and guidance by the Chaplains has a vital role on campus, although by its very nature a continuation of family pastoral care, it is more of a self-standing service.

On the basis that it represents the meeting of the most basic and essential of common human needs, the catering service should be organized in a way that pays due regard to the life-style of students. Thus the environmental layout of refectories should be geared to encouraging and not prohibiting social interaction; menus should be varied; and prices should be within the reach of all student users.

Integration of Theory and Practice

All courses should be encouraged to organize at least observational practical work for students so that they can sample 'the world of work' in a dialectical sense, and begin to reflect on issues concerning the integration of theory and practice.

Having been established in controversial circumstances during the 1980s, Enterprise in Higher Education programmes are now developing as integral parts of many academic courses. "Enterprise competencies in this context refer to a broad range of transferable skills which underpin effectiveness across all forms of activity and employment. In order to achieve our aim, the focus is particularly on curriculum development with a view to encouraging much more student-centred learning, and greater independence and autonomy from the teacher/lecturer." (Tate 1993).

It is argued convincingly that EHE case studies and live projects can bring a sharper lucidity to college-based theory.

The Research Dilemma

Unquestionably applied research is a core activity in order to obtain contract revenue from outside bodies, including government. However the trend towards 'selective research' which has 'marketable possibilities' must not lead to an unbridgeable dichotomy between those who carry out research and those who teach. Clearly, with the wide range of activities included in the 'old' and 'new' universities, many tutors will be content with a teaching role which does not formally demand a research output. However research and teaching do cross-fertilize one another and it is desirable that those tutors who wish to pursue research 'for its own sake' are enabled to do so. Students benefit from the additional richness of teaching material that automatically ensues.

University Teaching as a Trade

One of the greatest vulnerabilities of the student is to be part of a captive audience of a lecturer who simply cannot communicate. Consequently universities of the future should only employ lecturers who have undertaken recognized courses in 'the lecturer's trade'. Various initiatives have also started, including courses offering a postgraduate certificate in higher education teaching. In the interim, appraisal schemes should be implemented in the spirit that, largely through self-appraisal and evaluation with the assistance of students and peers, lecturers should continually work at improving lecturing and small group teaching skills. In-service training and short courses should be mounted in greater quantity to reflect the priority given to teaching skills.

Individual Student-Centred Practices

At a point when universities know they will have to subsist with a diminishing unit of resource, the means exist to maximize the quality of the student experience without an inflationary call on additional resources. These measures fall within the realm of attitudes and awareness. For instance prospective students must have access to educational guidance and counselling which is not imbued with economic vested interests. There is nothing so corrosive as a decision taken on an ill-advised basis to pursue a particular course. Indeed early disinterested guidance and counselling can ensure lower drop-out rates whatever course or university the student chooses.

As a joint exercise between Faculties, personal students services and academic registry, individualised assessments should be made available to students where appropriate. This would usually happen if the student had a special need arising from disability or had been removed from formal full-time education for a number of years. Action plans could then be devised by way of a 'contract' in which student and university staff were clear about mutual obligations, including any special equipment, examination arrangements, timetabling implications. It is likely that the proportion of students with significant disability in higher education will increase rapidly over the next few years, and all universities should develop a special needs protocol in preparation for this welcome and overdue progress.

Admission criteria should be as flexible as possible to reflect the principle that higher education is a right and not a privilege. If necessary, counselling feedback can be provided to prospective students where the risk of non-completion appears high. Active encouragement should also be given to those school-leavers who wish to defer their entry for a year, as this can often be consistent with adaptation to academic life.

All citizens should receive clear messages from their regional academic institutions that education is a lifelong process not confined to school age and young adulthood. Thus, be they married women, redundant workers, retired citizens, or just interested people, they should be encouraged to participate in foundation and bridging courses, part-time modes of study, outreach course centres, unassessed evening classes.

During the period of study, students should have the right to withdraw for a 'year out'. This could be in the form of related work activity, sabbatical service in the Students' Union/Representative Council, or just the gaining of wider life experience.

Furthermore, the principle of 'transferability' should always operate whereby, up to a certain stage, students may transfer between courses within the institution, between modes of study, or between universities. Clearly the 'Credit Accumulation and Transfer Scheme' will contribute greatly to this flexibility.

Students should be encouraged to internalize the principle that they should accept responsibility for their own learning. On the one hand, this is going to have to be an increasing expectation because of larger student cohorts and limits on the academic staff resources. On the other hand, the fundamental principles of learning recognize that true learning takes place, not through passive receipt of transmitted material, but through active and independent pursuit by the student. In addition to intellectual stimulation, campus life should offer students rich opportunities for development in the social, emotional and cultural spheres as well.

It is vital that a climate which rewards creativity and imaginative exploration is maintained, and that students do not receive confusing mixed messages implying a 'hidden curriculum' of narrow competitiveness. Neither should students feel that they are stereotyped by academic and administrative staff in terms of their gender, age, race or religion. Celebration of cultural and human diversity should always be the hallmark of university life. Interpersonal communication between staff and students should be at the level of adult to adult dialogue, and not paternalistic. Teachers should be open and willing to learn from student, as people who come to university with resources of their own to contribute. There should be general recognition that the process of real learning takes place through critical reflection, action and praxis. Students should never be viewed as empty vessels passively waiting to be filled with transmitted 'knowledge'. Universities in democratic societies represent no less than iconoclastic guardians of freedom of thought.

A Community Perspective
The higher education campus should be open and accessible and not steeped in detached mystification. People from the community should be able to enter the campus at all hours of the waking day to partake of taught courses, research, debates, social events or quiet reflection. The students and the wider community should, as a result, experience and enjoy a positive mutual respect and understanding. A university should be of the people and for the people.

The Measurement of 'Value-Added'
Since the argument has been sustained throughout this book that universities should be viewed as a public service with the widest possible access, it follows that funding must be predominantly from the public purse. Reciprocally, the institutions must be able to demonstrate their accountability, and provide tangible evidence of money well spent.

It has already been indicated that there are inherent difficulties in trying to measure accurately the process of value-added. While it is possible to compare the initial 'A' Level grades (or equivalent) of students with the classification of the final award, interpretation may be ambiguous. Does a high-achieving profile at entry tend to diminish automatically the apparent extent of the value-added by the academic experience? How can comparisons be drawn in a valid way between the profiles of school-leavers and those of the growing proportion of mature students whose entry may be based on very non-traditional qualifications.

Similar problems arise in relation to measurement of the income of the student before and after the course. What is being measured when the salary of the new graduate is taken into account? This form of measurement reflects not so much the value-added to the students by the educational experience but the perceived value attached to the academic qualification by the employer. It is difficult to assess what this approach achieves other than feedback about the market worthiness of the academic courses. This is of course useful information in terms of forward planning and curriculum development but it does not get to the heart of the quality of the student experience per se.

The most direct way to evaluate the content of the courses is to ask the students! Consequently there must be formal procedures built into the structures at several levels to ensure that this feedback happens. It has been suggested earlier that the staff/student consultative committee is a crucial element, whereby properly minuted evaluation is carried out of all aspects of academic courses, such as teaching standards, coherence of the course content, administrative efficiency, and basically whether the 'contract' of the course has been fulfilled to the mutual satisfaction of students and staff. This exercise can lead to improvements in the course delivery and teaching standards, with in-service training being provided at the very least should difficulties emerge in relation to standards of teaching. Furthermore it can reinforce the personal development of the student representatives as they carry out the demanding adult role of speaking on behalf of their peers and giving utterance to issues which at times must be delicate and problematic. It is often argued that students' perceptions of what constitute 'good' teaching can be distorted by their own prejudgements about their learning needs. For instance, a student who sees education as preparing in a regurgitative way for examinations will have different views on the methods used by the tutor than someone who enjoys small group discussion. While these points have some validity there is on the other hand a very strong likelihood that student representatives, if feedback from their peers has been properly sought, will normally be able to present a consensus view about 'good' teaching, and reciprocally will identify the features of a badly taught course.

At a global level, it is also desirable to invite all graduands to complete an anonymous individual survey questionnaire before departure, reflecting opinions on the quality of their courses, the availability and usefulness of support services, and future plans regarding employment. Such material can be of immense value to the academic policy and decision-making forums of the university. For instance if availability of library books is revealed as a major problem, there may be implications for future budgeting priorities. If access to computer services is problematic, there may be staffing issues that need to be addressed. Once again the positive message to students in carrying out these procedures is that they are being invited to contribute towards the future wellbeing of the university.

Personal Profiles

Although these forms of evaluation are useful, they do not represent profound and incisive measures of the quality of the 'value-added' and the nature of the transformation within the individual student. It could be therefore that a specially devised instrument of measurement is required. What would be the primary objective of such a measure? It would have to be capable of reflecting any changes which have taken place in the personal development of the students across a wide range of dimensions. These dimensions could be summarized as :

political awareness;
social confidence and skills;
cultural appreciation;
community involvement;
cognitive abilities;
attitudinal flexibility;
emotional harmony;
health and fitness.

This is not to imply some sort of prescription for a 'perfect citizen'. There would be no inbuilt value assumptions as to what constitutes 'good' or 'desirable' change in any of the dimensions. Rather it would represent an instrument by which the individual student could identify his or her individual stage of development at the point of entry onto the course and be given feedback as to the areas of personal growth. The most significant aspect of the measures would be that in their entirety they would represent the collective 'identity' of the students, and would be an important affirmation of the strengths and qualities making up that identity at this stage when the student is about to graduate and find a niche in wider society. It is important to stress that the scores would remain a strictly confidential matter between the student and the academic department and would only be made available in full or in part to employers or any other interested party with the explicit consent of the student. Essentially the record of the transformation would be a helpful and supportive feedback for the student and would provide invaluable data for the institution in terms of future policy planning and provision.

It is proposed therefore that universities could consider undertaking pilot projects to try to establish useful forms of measurement of personal development. This would mean selecting two groups for longitudinal study –

(a) a group of new entrants into university;
(b) a second group with similar profiles who opted to start their professional careers direct from school.

The differences in the scores would then indicate the areas in which the academic institutions tended to enhance personal development or not as the case may be, and provide direct comparison with young adults in full-time employment.

When considering the actual means of measurement, it is evident that traditional sociometric techniques or questionnaire surveys would not be sufficient to address the multiplicity of factors which are operant. Therefore some form of multi-level battery of measurements would have to be devised. Weinreich has been carrying out interesting work of direct relevance in investigating identity processes. He defines identify thus:

> One's identity is defined as the totality of one's self-construal, in which how one construes oneself in the present expresses the continuity between how one construes oneself as one was in the past and how one construes oneself as one aspires to be in the future. (P Weinrech 1989.)

Focusing specifically on ethnic identity he argues that no one universal theory can be constructed that will address all the complexities of states of identity. Therefore he argues for a 'metatheoretical' framework consisting of several perspectives. These include: the personal construct theory view of self as expounded by Kelly; psychodynamic developmental theory (eg Erikson); cognitive-affective consistency orientation (eg Rosenberg and Abelson) which examines the relationship of the self's cognitions of people and the affective connotations of these cognitions for the person. Symbolic interactionist theory (eg Goffman) offers the perspective that there is a social context to the 'self' and that individuals develop style of self-presentation and negotiations with others in terms of differing social contexts. Ancestry, progeny and kinship structures are also addressed by incorporating social anthropological perspectives (eg Rosaldo and Lamphere). From this meta-theoretical framework, theoretical postulates are derived about the constructs which people use to interpret and evaluate others and themselves within the social context:

> The application of this framework of concepts and postulates to empirical data collected using appropriately designed identity instruments enables the investigator to generate theoretical propositions about the socio-psychological processes of identity development in the socio-historical and biographical context under investigation. (P Weinreich 1989 p 53.)

Personalized concepts are then derived which act as the parameters of identity properties. And following idiographic analysis by means of a computer program, the parameters of identity structure for the individual can be delineated.

In practical terms, the undergraduates in the initial sample could be invited to take part in a longitudinal study whereby a baseline measure is recorded at the point of arrival at the institution and a follow-up exercise takes place at the stage of graduation.

By use of a 'user-friendly' computer program, these exercises could eventually be undertaken by all undergraduates quickly and efficiently as part of the accepted routine of the institution.

In effect they would become part of the mutually agreed 'contract' between the students and the universities of their choice in order to facilitate their personal development.

Less elaborated means are of course possible to provide students with personal profiles of achievement reflecting their development. Simple charts could be recorded on a continuous basis by the student and studies adviser denoting: academic achievements; social and cultural participation; special interest projects undertaken (eg EHE); extramural interests; practice placement experience; and perhaps self-assessment in terms of acquired skills and abilities. Students would then be able to draw on these profiles when applying for employment or postgraduate courses. A proforma example of a Profile of Achievement is provided in Appendix V.

Postscript

Momentous changes have taken place on the higher education landscape since the 1960s. With the removal of the binary line, mass higher education in a hybrid range of universities is now a reality, and student populations are not only growing but becoming ever more heterogeneous. While widened access is to be welcomes, giving new opportunities to hitherto disadvantaged people in our society, it is important that universities reflect long and hard on their fundamental objectives. The days of insulated elitism have long since passed, and universities perforce are much more accountable. At the same time, there is a cogent argument for retaining autonomy and academic freedom as much in the interests of wider society as for the benefit of the institutions themselves. Thus a careful balance has to be struck. In this book, an argument has been made that it is useful in this respect to consider the notion of 'value-added'. How is the student enriched as a person by entering the portals of higher education in preference to some other route? In what ways should universities seek to measure what they offer, so that students can have tangible evidence to offer in terms of furthering their careers, and wider society can be reassured that money from the public purse is being well spent?

As the new century nears, it is by confirming the ways in which they contribute to the personal development of students, beyond the mere acquisition of a qualification, that universities will affirm their validity and value for money.

Appendix 1

A Chronicle of British and Irish Universities

As indicated, British universities have been empowered since the Medieval Age to grant degrees. Initially Papal Bulls founded the institutions, to be later replaced by Royal Charters or Acts of Parliament. These conferred powers have given the universities a form of self-contained legal existence. The universities have also traditionally been afforded substantial autonomy in governing their own financial and academic affairs. Outlined below is a chronicle of British and Irish Universities which have come into existence since 1214.

Oxford	1214

granted privileges by the papal legate.

Cambridge	1318

recognized as a 'Studium generale' by Pope John XXII

St Andrews	1413

Papal Bull

Glasgow	1451

Papal Bull

Aberdeen	1494

Papal Bull

Edinburgh	1583

Royal Charter

University of Dublin	1591

(Trinity College Dublin) – Royal Charter

College of St Patrick Maynooth Ireland	1795

Act of Parliament

Durham	1832

an Act "to enable the Dean and Chapter of Durham to appropriate part of the property of their Church to the establishment of a university in connection therewith."

London	1836

Royal Charter

Queen's Colleges (Cork, Galway, Belfast)	1845
Royal Charter	
Catholic University of Ireland	1854
established by the Irish synod of Catholic Bishops	
Victoria (Owens College, Yorkshire College)	
Royal Charter (dismembered 1903/4)	1880
University of Wales	1893
(Aberystwyth, Bangor, Cardiff – Swansea added in 1920)	
Royal Charter	
Birmingham	1900
Royal Charter	
Liverpool	1903
Royal Charter	
Manchester	1903
Royal Charter	
Leeds	1904
Royal Charter	
Sheffield	1905
Royal Charter	
(Queen's University of Belfast	1908
(University College Cork	1908
(University College Galway	1908
(University College Dublin	1908
designated as 'Teaching Universities' under the	
Irish Universities Act 1908	
Bristol	1909
Royal Charter	
Reading	1926
Royal Charter	
Nottingham	1948
Royal Charter	
Southampton	1952
Royal Charter	
Hull	1954
Royal Charter	
Exeter	1955
Royal Charter	

Manchester Institute of Science & Technology
    Royal Charter as a college   1956
    adopted the title of University   1966
Leicester   1957
    Royal Charter
Sussex   1961
    Royal Charter
Keele   1962
    Royal Charter
Newcastle-upon-Tyne   1963
    under the Universities of Durham and
    Newcastle-upon-Tyne Act
York   1963
    Royal Charter
East Anglia   1964
    Royal Charter
Lancaster   1964
    Royal Charter
Strathclyde   1964
    Royal Charter
Essex   1965
    Royal Charter
Kent   1965
    Royal Charter
Warwick   1965
    Royal Charter
Aston   1966
    Charter granted by the Privy Council
Bath   1966
    Royal Charter
Bradford   1966
    Royal Charter
City   1966
    Royal Charter
Heriot-Watt   1966
    Royal Charter
Loughborough   1966
    Charter as a University of Technology

Surrey	1966
Royal Charter	
Dundee	1967
Royal Charter	
Royal College of Art	1967
Royal Charter (brought within the ambit of the University grants system on the recommendation of the Robbins Committee - 1963)	
Salford	1967
Royal Charter	
Stirling	1967
Royal Charter	
Cranfield Institute of Technology	1969
Royal Charter	
Open	1969
Royal Charter	
New University of Ulster	1971
Royal Charter	
Buckingham	1983
Royal Charter	
Ulster	1984
Royal Charter (merger of the New University of Ulster and the Ulster Polytechnic)	
Dublin City University	1989
by legislation	
University of Limerick	1989
by legislation	

(*Sources:*
(i) Commonwealth Universities Yearbook 1989 Vol 1 A-B The Association of Commonwealth Universities)
(ii) Atkinson A "Irish Education" Allen Figgis Dublin 1969)

New universities (37 polytechnics which have assumed university status since September 1992):

Anglia Polytechnic University (Chelmsford)
Bournemouth University
University of Brighton

University of Central England in Birmingham (Perry Barr)
City of London Polytechnic
Coventry University
University of Derby
University of East London
University of Glamorgan (Pontypridd)
Glasgow Polytechnic/The Queen's College
University of Greenwich
University of Hertfordshire (Hatfield)
University of Huddersfield
University of Humberside (Hull)
Kingston University
University of Central Lancashire (Preston)
Leeds Metropolitan University
De Mortfort University (Leicester)
Liverpool John Moores University
Manchester Metropolitan University
Middlesex University
Napier University (Edinburgh)
University of North London
University of Northumbria at Newcastle
Nottingham Trent University
Oxford Brookes University
University of Paisley (SW Glasgow)
University of Portsmouth
University of Plymouth
The Robert Gordon University (Aberdeen)
Sheffield Hallam University
South Bank University
Staffordshire University (Stoke-on-Trent)
University of Sunderland
University of Teeside (Middlesborough)
Thames Valley University
University of the West of England, Bristol
University of Westminster
University of Wolverhampton

(*Source:* The Higher Times Education Supplement 2 October 1992, pps 22,23)

Appendix II

Ratio of First-Time Entrants to Population (1988)

	Non-university tertiary			Higher education university			Total		
	Men & Women	Men	Women	Men & Women	Men	Women	Men & Women	Men	Women
A									
Japan	26.8	16.4	37.7	24.6	34.5	14.1	51.4	51.0	51.9
United States	22.0	18.3	25.8	47.5	49.4	45.6	69.5	67.7	71.5
B									
Australia	-	-	-	50.4	48.8	52.0	-	-	-
Denmark	15.5	11.9	19.5	27.6	29.8	25.2	43.1	41.7	44.7
Finland	24.0	16.5	31.9	28.0	29.0	27.0	52.1	45.5	58.9
France	13.3	-	-	23.1	-	-	36.4	-	-
Italy	1.0	0.8	1.1	27.3	27.7	27.0	28.3	28.5	28.1
New Zealand	-	-	. -	18.6	20.2	17.0	-	-	-
Norway	-	-	-	15.6	15.1	16.1	-	-	-
Spain	-	-	-	36.6	35.2	37.9	36.6	35.3	38.0
Sweden	36.1	33.6	38.8	13.7	13.7	13.6	48.9	46.5	51.4
Turkey	2.4	3.3	1.4	12.1	15.6	8.4	14.5	19.0	9.9
United Kingdom	6.2	6.1	6.4	15.0	16.0	14.0	21.2	22.1	20.4
C									
Austria	4.4	2.8	6.2	18.1	18.1	18.1	22.6	20.9	24.3
Belgium	-	-	-	19.8	21.9	17.7	-	-	-
Germany	9.2	7.2	11.4	19.5	22.6	16.2	28.7	29.8	27.5
Ireland	15.1	16.1	14.1	15.8	15.6	15.9	30.9	31.8	30.0
Luxembourg	5.1	-	-	10.3	-	-	15.4	-	-
Netherlands	18.3	19.5	17.1	12.3	14.0	10.6	29.9	32.6	27.0
Portugal	NA	NA	NA	16.0	NA	NA	NA	NA	NA
Switzerland	10.4	13.1	7.6	12.3	14.6	9.8	22.7	27.7	17.4

Ratio of first-time entrants to population (1988)

(*Source:* Education at a glance OECD Indicators 1992.)

Appendix III

International Committees at the University of Ulster

Terms of Reference

1. To encourage social contact between individual overseas students and families in the local community.

2. To enrich the experience of the overseas students through contact with aspects of Northern Ireland's social and cultural life.

3. To promote international understanding, eg the organising of special evenings on national customs, food, drink, costume, dance.

4. To enhance Northern Ireland's reputation internationally by extending our communication networks with overseas countries.

5. To give visibility to the University of Ulster's overseas reputation.

Appendix IV

Special Needs Protocol

University of Ulster

Guidance & Welfare Officer
Student Services
Cromore Road
Coleraine
Co Londonderry
BT52 1SA

Tel: 0265 44141 extn 4136

PART I
(to be completed by student)

Name	Date of birth
Address	Tel:
	Please tick Male ☐ Female ☐
	Post code
	Are you registered disabled? Yes ☐ No ☐

Nature of special need (please specify):

COURSES applied for at the University of Ulster:

First choice [ ]   Campus [ ]

Second choice [ ]   Campus [ ]

Current offer
(please tick)

Unconditional ☐	First choice ☐	Second choice ☐
Conditional ☐	First choice ☐	Second choice ☐
Waiting list ☐	First choice ☐	Second choice ☐
Not known yet ☐		

ACCOMMODATION :   Do you intend to apply for campus accommodation   Yes ☐ No ☐
(please tick)

If yes, do you require: wheelchair access? ☐
Ground floor? ☐
other special arrangements? ☐

Please outline any other requirements you may have for accommodation:

PART I (CONTINUED)

ASSISTANCE - are you likely to require assistance with any of the following (please tick):

personal care	☐
at mealtimes	☐
with cooking	☐
with cleaning	☐
with laundry	☐
with shopping	☐
getting around the campus	☐

EQUIPMENT

Do you need to use specialized equipment for study purposes   No ☐   Yes ☐
Please specify:

1	4
2	5
3	6

Please list any equipment which you intend bringing to university with you:

1	4
2	5
3	6

ADDITIONAL INFORMATION

Please add anything else which you feel is important to your circumstances and would be useful for us to know.

Signature _____   Date _____

Value-Added

PART II - ASSESSMENT
(to be completed by staff)

Name	Date of birth :
Home address :	Term-time address :
Post code ————	Post code ————
Tel :	Tel :

1. ACCESS

    Car park space ☐   Escort services ☐   Adapted toilets ☐

    Additional information :

2. ACADEMIC/STUDY NEEDS

    Special arrangements for :

Timetable ☐	Teaching areas ☐	Educational aids ☐
Reading ☐	Writing ☐	Hearing ☐
Computer ☐	Library ☐	Industrial placement ☐

    Additional information :

PART II (CONTINUED)

3. ACCOMMODATION

At home ☐   on-campus ☐   off-campus ☐

On-campus accommodation needs :

Alarm system ☐   Telephone ☐   Drug storage fridge ☐   Wheelchair access ☐

Clinical waste disposal ☐   Special adaptations ☐   Own bathroom/toilet ☐

Additional information :

4. PERSONAL CARE

Assistance with :

Cooking ☐   Shopping ☐   Cleaning ☐   Personal hygiene ☐

Medical/nursing services ☐   Laundry ☐   Mealtimes ☐

Additional information :

Value-Added

<table>
<tr><td colspan="2" align="center">PART II CONTINUED</td></tr>
</table>

5. FINANCIAL

Equipment grants:	applied for	Yes ☐	No ☐
	approved	Yes ☐	No ☐
	received	Yes ☐	No ☐
Disability allowance:	applied for	Yes ☐	No ☐
	approved	Yes ☐	No ☐
	received	Yes ☐	No ☐
Support from voluntary bodies:	applied for	Yes ☐	No ☐
	approved	Yes ☐	No ☐
	received	Yes ☐	No ☐

Additional information :

6. EQUIPMENT

List of equipment which may be required on short term loan or for continued use from the University.

1	4
2	5
3	6

Additional information :

PART II CONTINUED

---

7. SOCIAL AND CULTURAL

List the social activities in which the student would like to continue or participate:

1	4
2	5
3	6

Additional information :

Signature of Assessor _____ Date _____

Value-Added

PART III - ACTION PLAN						
NAME		DATE OF BIRTH	SENIOR COURSE TUTOR		STUDIES ADVISER	
DATE	NEEDS IDENTIFIED	ACTION TAKEN		OUTCOME	REVIEW DATE	SIGNATURE
ACCESS						
ACADEMIC/STUDY NEEDS						
ACCOMMODATION						

PERSONAL CARE

FINANCIAL

SOCIAL CULTURAL

SIGNATURE OF ASSESSOR ———————— DATE

SIGNATURE OF STUDENT ———————— DATE

Page 7

Appendix V

Proforma
Profile of Achievement

Student's Name:

Course:

Year One/Two

Academic Record:

Subjects taken; examination results; seminar papers presented; quality of participation in discussion groups. Learning skills groups attended.

Social Activities:

Sport and recreation; development of existing interests; discovery of new skills. Travel undertaken. Responsibilities undertaken, eg living away from home. Clubs and societies joined, and offices held. Participation in Students' Union activities.

Cultural Activities:

Horizons broadened through internal and external involvement in musical, literary, historical, scientific societies, film societies, concerts, festivals.

Political Development:

Involvement in debating societies; exploration of issues, re: human and welfare rights; social policy; feminism, racism.

Practical Work:

Observation visits and course placements undertaken. Learning points arising. Enterprise in Higher Education projects; assessment of skills developed – communication skills; relationship building; administrative and organisational abilities; compilation of agendas; chairing meetings; taking minutes, forward planning.

Community Work:

Voluntary or part-time paid work undertaken, eg schools liaison visits; mental handicap day centres; service to older people or disabled people.

Studies Adviser's Additional Comments:

Student's Self-Assessment:

Student's Name:

Course:

Final Year

Academic Record:

Quality of dissertation; research skills demonstrated; capacity to develop cogent arguments. Evidence of independent study strengths; involvement in syndicate groups and peer support groups. Provision of academic peer support to junior students. Subjects taken for Finals; analysis of results in terms of prior expectations, strengths demonstrated.

Social Activities:

Evidence of collegiate participation as a senior student eg senior resident student in Halls of Residence; student representative in staff/student consultative committee or course review committee. Quality of relationship with studies adviser; ability to enter into adult to adult dialogue. Use made of support services, eg careers advisory service; learning skills groups.

Cultural Activities:

Involvement in the organisation of societies, internal or external, eg music, science, humanities, art, drama.

Political Development:

Identification of any avenues of interest pursued, eg membership of Amnesty International, articles for journals on social, political or economic issues.

Practical Work:

Enterprise in Higher Education projects; identification of specific transferable skills developed, eg interpersonal, administrative, leadership, forward planning, goal-setting.

Community Work:

Involvement in International Committees; social, cultural and educational visits to schools; hospital voluntary work; community care (voluntary or part-time employed).

Studies Adviser's Additional Comments:

Student's Self-Assessment:

References

A

ALLEN M, *The Goals of Universities*, SRHE and Open University Press, 1988.

ARBLASTER A, *Academic Freedom*, Penguin Education, 1974.

ATKINSON N, *Irish Education – a history of educational institutions*, Allen Figgis, Dublin, 1969.

B

BAGLEY B & CHALLIS B, *Inside Open Learning*, Further Education Staff College, 1985.

BALDWIN J AND WILLIAMS H, *Active Learning – a trainer's guide*, Blackwell Education, 1988.

BARNARD H C, *A History of English Education from 1760*, University of London Press, 1969.

BARNES J AND BARR N, *Strategies for Higher Education – an Alternative White Paper*, Aberdeen University Press, 1988.

BARROW J C, *Fostering cognitive development of students*, Jossey-Bass, 1986.

BASSEY M, *A Challenge to the Ideology of the Education Reform Bill*, Trent Polytechnic, 1987.

BIRCH W, *The Challenge to Higher Education – reconciling responsibilities to scholarship and to society*, SRHE and Open University Press, 1988.

BRONOWSKI J, *The Ascent of Man*, BBC, 1973.

BROSAN G, PARKER C, LAYARD R, VENABLES P, WILLIAMS G, *Patterns and Fallacies in Higher Education*, Penguin, 1971.

BROWN G and ATKINS M, *Effective Teaching in Higher Education*, Methuen, 1988.

C

CANTOR L, *Vocational Education and Training in the Developed World – a Comparative Study*, Routledge, 1989.

CARSWELL J, *Government and the Universities in Britain – 1960-80*, Cambridge University Press, 1985.

CAUL B P, *Promoting Independent Learning and Maintaining Quality in Mass Higher Education*, 8th International Conference of University Administrators, Singapore, January 1993.

CAUL B P, 'Support Services for Overseas Students' in CALLAN H (ed), *Overseas Students – a Guide to Practice*, UKCOSA, 1991.

CAUL B P and WILSON N, *The Use of Hypertext in Students' Self-paced Learning*, SRHE Conference, Nottingham University, December 1992.

CAVE M, HANNEY S, KOGAN M, and TREVETT G, *The Use of Performance Indicators in Higher Education: a critical analysis of developing practice*, Jessica Kingsley Publishers, 1988.

COHEN A and GARNER N, *Readings on the History of Educational Thought*, University of London Press, 1967.

COHEN L H (ed), *Life Events and Psychological Functioning*, Sage Publications, 1988.

COMMONWEALTH UNIVERSITIES YEARBOOK, 1989, Vol 1 A-B, The Association of Commonwealth Universities, 1989.

COOLAHAN J, *Irish Education – History and Structure*, Institute of Public Administration, 1981.

COOMBE LODGE REPORT, *Developing a Policy for Recruiting Overseas Students*, Part I Vol 17 No 11, 1985.

COWLEY J, KAYE A, MAYO M and THOMPSON M, *Community or Class Struggle*, Stage I, 1977.

CURTIS S J, *History of Education in Great Britain*, University Tutorial Press.

CURTIS S J and BOULTWOOD M E A, *A short history of Educational Ideas*, University Tutorial Press, 1961.

D

DALE R, ESLAND G and MacDONALD M, (eds) *Schooling and Capitalism – a sociological reader*, Routledge & Kegan Paul, 1976.

DELAMONT S, *Knowledgeable Women – Structuralism and the reproduction of elites*, Routledge, 1989.

DILLON R S and SCHMECK R R (eds), *Individual Differences in Cognition*, Vol 1, Academic Press, 1983.

DOIDGE J & WHITCHURCH, *Total Quality Matters*, CUA Good Practice Series No 13, 1993.

DOWLING P J A, *History of Irish Education – Study in Conflicting Loyalties*, The Mercier Press, 1971.

DURCAN T J, *History of Irish Education from 1800*, Dragon Books, 1972.

E

ENTWHISTLE N, *The Impact of Teaching on Learning Outcomes in Higher Education*, CVCP/USDU, 1992.

ERICKSON F and SCHULTZ J, *The Counsellor as Gate Keeper*, Academic Press, 1982

ERIKSON E H, *Childhood and Society*, New York:Norton, 1963.

F

FELDMAN KA (ed), *College and Student*, Pergamon Press, 1977.

FO D, 'Singing in the Dark Times', *Observer*, 24th April, 1983, p 32.

FREIRE P, *Education for Critical Consciousness*, Gheed and Ward, 1974.

G

GALE A and EDWARDS J A, *Physiological Correlates of Human Behaviour – Attention and Performance*, Vol 2, Academic Press Inc, 1973.

GARDNER H, *Arts, Mind and Brain*, Basic Books, 1982.

GILBERT J (ed), *Staying the Course – How to Survive Higher Education*, Kogan Page, 1979.

GOUGH I, *The Political Economy of the Welfare State*, MacMillan Press, 1979.

GRAVES N, *The Education Crisis: which way now?*, Christopher Helm, 1988.

H

HALDANE Viscount, *Universities and National Life*, John Murray, London, 1912.

HENWORTH, *University Appointments Boards – A Report by The Rt Hon The Lord Henworth*, London, HMSO, 1964.

HILLS P J, *Study Courses and Counselling*, SRHE, 1979.

HOPPER E (ed), *Readings in the Theory of Educational Systems*, Hutchinson & Co, 1971.

I

ILLICH I, *Tools for Conviviality*, Calder & Boyars, London, 1973.

J

JOHNSTON J, *How many miles to Babylon?*, Hamish Hamilton, 1974.

JONES H A and WILLIAMS K E, *Adult Students and Higher Education*, Advisory Council for Adult and Continuing Education, 1979.

JONES K, *Collatoration or Competition*, Corporate Planning Forum, CUA, 1993.

JONES S, *Opportunities and Provisions for Students with Physical Disabilities in Higher Education*, in EDUCARE – National bureau for Handicapped Students - No 31 June, 1988.

K

KEDOURIE E, *Diamonds into Glass – the Government and the Universities*, Centre for Policy Studies, 1988.

KRUEGER D W, *Success and the Fear of Success in Women*, The Free Press, 1984.

L

LAWSON J and SILVER H, *A Social History of Education in England*, Methuen, 1973.

LEAHEY T H, *A History of Psychology – Main Currents in Psychological Thought*, Prentice-Hall, 1987.

LEE C L, *The People's Universities of the USSR*, Greenwood Press, 1988.

LEWIS I, *The Student Experience of Higher Education*, Croom Helm, 1984.

LISTON D P, *Capitalist Schools – Explanations and Ethics in Radical Studies of Schooling*, Routledge, 1988.

LODGE D, *Nice Work*, Secker & Warburg, 1988.

LOWRY R J (ed), *Dominance, Self-esteem, Self-actualisation: Germinal Papers of A H Maslow*, Wadsworth Publishing Company, 1973.

M

MASLOW A H, *The Farther Reaches of Human Nature*, Viking Press, 1971.

MASLOW A H, *Towards a Psychology of Being*, van Nostrand Reinhold Co, New York, 1968.

MEREDEEN S, *Study for Survival and Success*, Paul Chapman Publishing Co, 1988.

MONTEFIORE A (ed), *Neutrality and Impartiality – University and Political Commitments*, Cambridge University Press, 1975.

MORRIS M and GRIGGS C (eds), *Education – the wasted years? 1973-1986*, The Falmer Press, 1988.

McALLISTER W J, *The growth of Freedom in Education*, Constable & Co, 1931.

McCRINDLE J and ROWBOTHAM S (eds), *Dutiful Daughters*, Penguin, 1983.

McLELLAN G, *Marxism and the Methodologies of History*, Verso Editions and NLB, 1981.

N

NATIONAL UNION OF STUDENTS, *Students' Charter*, NUS, 1993.

NEWMAN J H, *On the Scope and Nature of University education*, Dent:London (1852) Everyman's Library, Reprinted 1965.

NICHOLAS E J, *Issues in Education: a Comparative Analysis*, Harper & Row 1983.

NUNN Sir P, *Education – Its Data and Principles*, Edward Arnold, 1970.

O

OSBORNE R D, CORMACK R J and MILLER R L, *Education and Policy in Northern Ireland*, Policy Research Institute, 1987.

P

POLLARD A, PURVIS J and WALFORD G (eds), *Education, Training and the New Vocationalism*, Open University Press, 1988.

R

RAAHEIM K, WANKOWSKI J AND RADFORD J, *Helping Students to Learn*, SRHE & Open University Press, 1991.

ROGERS J, *Adults Learning*, Penguin, 1971.

RUDDICK J, *Learning through Small Group Discussion*, SRHE, 1979.

S

SHARAN S and SHARAN Y, *Small-group teaching*, Educational Technology Publications, 1976.

SCOTT T, *The Crisis of the University*, Croom Helm, 1984.

SHIPMAN M, *Education as a Public Service*, Harper & Row, 1984.

SMITH R M, *Learning how to Learn*, Open University Press, 1988.

STERNBERG R J (ed), *Mechanisms of Cognitive Development*, W H Freeman & Co, 1984.

T

TATE A, *Enterprise in Higher Education: Two Years Old*, UU Alumni News, Issue No 3, April 1993.

THOMAS K, 'Being in a Minority: the Experience of 1st Year Female Physics Students and 1st year Male Arts Students', *Report on Proceedings of the 1986 International Conference on The First Year Experience, (7-11th July 1986)*, Newcastle-upon-Tyne, England, Newcastle-upon-Tyne Polytechnic/SRHE, 1986.

THOMPSON E P, *Warwick University Ltd*, Penguin Education, 1970.

THOMPSON K, *Education and Philosophy*, Basil Blackwell, 1980.

TREVELYAN G M, *English Social History – a Survey of Six Centuries*, Book Club Associates, 1973.

TRUSCOT B, *Redbrick University*, Pelican, 1951.

TYLER L E, *The Work of the Counsellor*, Prentice Hall, 1969.

U

UK COUNCIL FOR OVERSEAS STUDENT AFFAIRS, *Towards a Policy on International Education*, UKCOSA, 1986.

UK COUNCIL FOR OVERSEAS STUDENT AFFAIRS, *International Comparisons in Overseas Affairs*, UKCOSA, 1986.

UK COUNCIL FOR OVERSEAS STUDENT AFFAIRS, *Overseas Students – Destination UK?*, UKCOSA, 1987.

UK COUNCIL FOR OVERSEAS STUDENT AFFAIRS, *The Teaching and Tutoring of Overseas Studies*, UKCOSA, 1985.

UK COUNCIL FOR OVERSEAS STUDENT AFFAIRS, *Overseas Students - who learns what?*, UKCOSA, 1985.

V

VADAS JE, *Interactive Videodisc for Management Training in a Classroom Environment*, IBM Corporate Management Development, 1984.

VAUGHAN T, *Education and the Aims of Counselling – a European Perspective*, Basil Blackwell, 1975.

W

WARNOCK M, *A Common Policy for Education*, Oxford University Press, 1988.

WATTS A G, LAW B and FAWCETT B, 'Some Implications for Guidance Practice', in WATTS A G, SUPER D E & KIDD J M (eds), *Career Development in Britain*, Careers Research & Advisory Centre, Hobsons Press, 1981.

WEINREICH P, 'Variations in Ethnic Identity: Identity Structure Analysis' in LIEBKIND K (ed), *New Identities in Europe: Immigrant Ancestry and the Ethnic Identity of Youth*, Gower Press in print, 1989.

WERTSCH J V (ed), *Culture, Communication and Cognition*, Cambridge University Press, 1985.

WRIGHTSMAN L S, Personality Development in Adulthood, Sage Publications, 1988.

Index